£50
80P

At Day's End

At Day's End
Book-Related Activities for Small Groups

Harriet R. Kinghorn
River Heights Elementary School
East Grand Forks, Minnesota

and

Fay Hill Smith
Drayton Public School
Drayton, North Dakota

Illustrations by Myke Knutson

1988

Libraries Unlimited, Inc.   Englewood, Colorado

LIBRARIES UNLIMITED, INC.
P.O. Box 3988
Englewood, Colorado 80155-3988

Library of Congress Cataloging-in-Publication Data

Kinghorn, Harriet R., 1933-
    At day's end : book-related activities for small groups / Harriet
R. Kinghorn and Fay Hill Smith ; illustrations by Myke Knutson.
    xxii, 235 p. 22x28 cm.
    Includes bibliographies and index.
    ISBN 0-87287-654-3
    1. Activity programs in education.   2. Creative activities and
seat work.   3. Children--Books and reading.   4. Interdisciplinary
approach in education.   I. Smith, Fay Hill.   II. Title.
LB1027.25.K56   1988
372.5--dc19   88-22491
                                           CIP

CONTENTS

PREFACE

If you remember your childhood doubtless you also remember the deadly hour of 3:00 o'clock on all those school-day afternoons—at the ends of days full of numbers and words and facts, of spelling and reading and calculating, of deciding between *who* and *whom*, *was* and *were*, *divisor* and *dividend*, of dittoes and workbooks and exercises and recitations. You remember the frenetic efforts of the school to give you all the knowledge and information and skill that your future would require, in school days that were both too short and too long. You remember 3:00 o'clock (or whatever hour it was in your school)—an hour or a half-hour before it was time to go home—how tired you were, how restless, how at odds you were with everyone and everything, how you craved action or excitement. Like Huckleberry Finn, you wanted to go somewhere and you didn't care where. Maybe, in your frustration, you told the teacher exactly what you thought of her rules and regulations; maybe you threw a spit ball at someone you were tired of; or maybe you spent the last half-hour of the school day poised on the edge of your seat, feet ready, muscles tensed, ready for the word that would free you for another day. You suffered the misery of student burn-out.

If you are a teacher you know the bitter taste of a burnt-out day, you know the frustrations of that last half-hour of the day, when you become more warden than teacher, more monster than mentor. Perhaps you have wished (on your way home) that your school would simply decide to trash that last half hour of the day; after all, little good, precious little learning, ever occurs then; it could be dispensed with. But then, you think, the pressure to cover everything—reading, writing, math, science, social studies—would intensify, the day would become even more frenetic; and the burn-out would occur a half-hour earlier—at 2:30 instead of 3:00—for both teacher and students.

The authors of this book were children once; they have been teachers even longer. They know all too well, at first hand, the woes of the end of the day. In casual conversations and workshops, they have heard other teachers wish for something to do, something to fill the dead end of the day, some learning experience, upbeat and positive, that would send children home looking forward to coming back on the next day. They have designed this book to fill that need.

The book consists of thirteen units, each dealing with a specific topic, and a section of general materials that can be used with any or all of the units. Each unit presents a variety of activities—reading, writing, drawing, sculpting, calculating, measuring—and a bibliography of children's books on the topic of the unit.

The units of this book are for the end of the day, though they can be used at any time, to supplement or complement the curriculum. They are designed to foster independence and a fascination with learning, to fill that last half-hour of the day with both pleasure and purpose, while enhancing the students' skills of observation, reading, writing, creating, discovering. They are designed to send students home in the afternoon with the same excitement that they arrived with in the morning, to share their discoveries or their creations with the members of their families.

These units are flexible. They can be used at any time; they can be adapted to suit the special needs of any classroom; they can be supplemented by the teacher's own materials or activities. They are divers, calling upon the skills of various subjects—language arts, mathematics, social studies, science, art.

The fun begins when the teacher announces the "Topic of the Week," and sets the students to reading on the topic. (Of course, a topic can last longer than a week, could even be a "topic of the month.") Students and teacher then discuss the topic, sharing information already gathered, revealing the questions they hope to answer in the activities that will follow. These questions can be as wide-ranging as (on the topic of birds), "Where do eagles build their nests?" and "What are feathers for?" They can be as spontaneous as "I wonder what the smallest bird in the world is."

The teacher then distributes activity sheets and file folders to keep them in, and reads through the activity sheets with the students pausing to explain and answer questions. Early enough in the day to allow students to plan their activities, the teacher asks students to designate the activities they will engage in, on the sign-up sheet (in the "Sample Forms" section). When the teacher has had an opportunity to note the number of students who have designated the various activities, the students are assigned locations in the classroom where specific activities will be pursued. Four students per activity at any given time is maximum; students will have opportunities to work on several while the topic is considered, including activities of their own design, which can be arranged by contract. Students sign up every day for a different activity as the week progresses, making their choices and thereby making a commitment to the activity. The student who chooses to work on an art project today—a clay sculpture of a bird (from the "Birds" unit), a model of an island in a plastic-plate sea ("Islands")—tomorrow may choose to write a "tangled tale" about a hard-working robin or to interview a fellow student who has researched the Audubon Society or to search for islands on the globe.

At the designated time—say, a half-hour before the end of the day—the students read their task sheets, gather the materials they need, and proceed to the location of their chosen activity. The teacher becomes a floating supervisor, circulating among the groups, encouraging and discussing their work.

By the end of the week or whatever period has been set aside for the topic, the students will have completed several activities; they will have engaged in research, writing, artistic expression; they will be surprised and pleased with how much they know about the topic of the week. They will be pleased that they have chosen the methods and terms of their learning, that they have followed their natural curiosity and thereby achieved something important. If the teacher has chosen to engage parents and families in these day's end activities, by using the letter to parents in the "Sample Forms" section and subsequently encouraging the students to involve their parents in their daily activities, then what began as a modest effort to salvage the end of the day can engage the interest and attention of a community of young scholars and their families.

Each of the topics includes a "culminating activity," which may serve to lend a sense of closure to the unit. The satisfaction with a topic completed—researched, written about, represented in sculpture or drawing or painting—may prove infectious, may very well generate an excitement that will carry over into the next week, to the next topic of the week. These little projects are likely to become the most satisfactory part of the students' day; the end of the day—formerly wasted, frustrating, unsatisfactory for teachers and students alike—is likely to be the part of the day that students anticipate with enthusiasm. If they head home in the afternoon wishing the day were longer, then every part of the school day will bask in the glow of their enthusiasm. It is when students feel that way about it that school truly becomes a place of learning.

ACKNOWLEDGMENTS

The authors wish to express their appreciation to Dale Taylor, Jill Skalicky, Brenda Leigh, Mary Weaver, Marcia Dietrich, Don Garnaas, and Julie Weber for their help, suggestions, and support while writing and testing this book.

SAMPLE FORMS

LETTER TO PARENTS

Dear Parents,

    Our current topic for study is _____.
We would greatly appreciate it if you could help your child find information—by sharing things that you know, by reading together, by being sure that your child is able to get to the library.

    Your child might share the learning with you by telling at least one thing about the topic each day. Mealtime is often a good time for sharing.

                               Thank you,

SIGN-UP SHEET

Sign up for the activity you want to do today.

AREA I. _____
(Activity)

1. _____

2. _____

3. _____

4. _____

AREA V. _____
(Activity)

1. _____

2. _____

3. _____

4. _____

AREA II. _____
(Activity)

1. _____

2. _____

3. _____

4. _____

AREA VI. _____
(Activity)

1. _____

2. _____

3. _____

4. _____

AREA III. _____
(Activity)

1. _____

2. _____

3. _____

4. _____

AREA VII. _____
(Activity)

1. _____

2. _____

3. _____

4. _____

AREA IV. _____
(Activity)

1. _____

2. _____

3. _____

4. _____

AREA VIII. _____
(Activity)

1. _____

2. _____

3. _____

4. _____

CONTRACT (for Students)

Name: _____   Date: _____

Approved by: _____   Date: _____

Title of Activity: _____

Materials needed for activity: _____

_____

_____

My plans for independent project:

_____

_____

_____

_____

_____

Date I would like to complete my project: _____

Comments about my completed project: Picture of Project

_____

_____

_____

_____

_____

_____

_____

OBSERVE AND RECORD, BE A REPORTER (Homework)

Name _____

Newspaper reporters look for facts: what was seen, when it was seen, where it was seen. Look for items, pictures, and objects that relate to the topic. Draw a picture of what you saw and answer the questions below each picture. If you find more than four items, use the back of this sheet of paper, or another sheet.

WHAT: _____

WHEN: _____

WHERE: _____

WHAT: _____

WHEN: _____

WHERE: _____

WHAT: _____

WHEN: _____

WHERE: _____

WHAT: _____

WHEN: _____

WHERE: _____

SUPPLEMENTARY MATERIALS AND ACTIVITIES

Crossword puzzles

Mad Libs

Science kits

Spelling bees (vocabulary)

Filmstrips

Books

Tapes

Chalkboard activities

Research activities

Activity books

Poetry (to read and write)

Plays

Math activities

Career activities

Arts and crafts

Cooking

Commercial games

Computer software

Teaching pictures

Puppets

Flannelboard activities

Creative writing

Textbooks

OTHERS:

_____

_____

_____

_____

About Research

NOTES TO THE TEACHER

OBJECTIVES

To teach students the basic procedures of research.

To help students learn about reference sources.

To help students understand how to organize and apply information.

MATERIALS

Pencils, large (12" x 18") construction paper, 9" x 12" pieces of construction paper, staplers, glue, scissors, lined paper, crayons and markers.

TOPIC OF THE WEEK

This introductory activity is to be used with the class as a whole as an introduction to the unit. To allow the students time to read and gather information, it should be used a day or more before they go to Day's End Areas.

(Do the last part of this activity together. Let the students brainstorm for ideas.

If the children do not know how to use the library, they need to receive instruction and practice before continuing with this and succeeding units.

The first research report will be a large group activity. All the students will write a report on the subject of *Giraffes*.)

DAY'S END AREAS

Session One (Teacher Task Sheet)

The teacher will guide the children in making research report folders, will read aloud to the children about the topic, and will instruct them in filling out research cards.

Session Two (Teacher Task Sheet)

The teacher will read aloud from two media sources after which the students will prepare research cards.

Session Three (Teacher Task Sheet)

The teacher will instruct the students in the basics of writing paragraphs and will help them write outlines.

Session Four (Teacher Task Sheet)

The teacher will supervise the children during the actual writing of the reports.

Session Five (Teacher Task Sheet)

The teacher will instruct the children about the location and organization of the Day's End Areas and the behavior that is expected there. A sign-up sheet will be used.

Session Five (Student Task Sheet)

The children will color, cut out, and assemble giraffe models.
(Duplicate the giraffe parts on yellow paper.)

Individual Research Report (Student Task Sheet)

The children will use *Hobbies* as their topic and do individual research reports.
(This will take more than one session, but is preparation for doing the needed research for subsequent units.)

CULMINATING ACTIVITY

The students may share their individual research reports along with any illustrations or objects that they may have made or acquired about the subject.

BIBLIOGRAPHY

Green, C., and W. Standford. *The Giraffes*. Minneapolis, Minn.: Crestwood House, 1987.

Kilpatrick, Cathy. *Giraffes*. East Sussex, England: Wayland Publishers, 1980.

Name _____

TOPIC OF THE WEEK

Use a dictionary to learn the meaning of the word *research*. Write it below. _____

_____

_____

What words do you associate with the word *research*?

_____   _____

_____   _____

_____   _____

_____   _____

_____   _____

_____   _____

Think of times when research might be necessary. For example, when might a scientist find it necessary to research for information? List your ideas below.

_____

_____

_____

_____

_____

_____

_____

_____

_____

_____

_____

_____

DAY'S END AREAS

SESSION ONE

Materials
Large sheets (12" x 18") of construction paper (1 per child), construction paper, staplers, glue, research card sheets, pencils, scissors.

Activity
1. The children will make research folders as follows. You might want to have a sample ready to show them.

   a. Fold a large sheet of construction paper in half to make a folder.

   b. Fold a smaller sheet of construction paper in half.

   c. Staple the sides of the paper to form a pocket.

   d. Glue this pocket inside the folded construction paper; place it at the bottom on the left side of the folder.

   e. Have the children each cut out four research cards and place them in the pockets.

2. Read aloud to the class from a book about giraffes.

3. The children will each write "The Giraffe" as the topic on a research card. They will then write their names. They will fill in the source of information (the book from which you read). They will then write in the space provided on the card the important information learned from hearing the material that you read.

   Discuss the fact that they should write in their own words, but accurately. Tell them that when doing research, they may need to check for accuracy in numbers, names, etc. by looking back at the material. Discuss with them what they found important and why.

RESEARCH CARD

TOPIC: _____ RESEARCHER: _____

SOURCE OF INFORMATION (The title of the book and the page numbers)

_____

_____

_____

IMPORTANT INFORMATION:

_____

_____

_____

_____

_____

RESEARCH CARD

TOPIC: _____ RESEARCHER: _____

SOURCE OF INFORMATION (The title of the book and the page numbers)

_____

_____

_____

IMPORTANT INFORMATION:

_____

_____

_____

_____

_____

SESSION TWO

Materials
Pencil, research cards

Activity
1. Read aloud to the class from another book that provides information about giraffes.

2. Have the students fill out research cards as they did in the first session.

3. Tell them that the information that they are gathering will be used to write reports.

4. Read aloud an article about giraffes from an encyclopedia.

5. The students will again prepare research cards on which they record the information learned from this source.

SESSION THREE

Materials
Pencils, blank outlines

Activity
1. Discuss with the students the basics of writing a paragraph (main idea, supporting details, etc.).

2. Discuss with them the information that they have gathered. Help them organize it into general ideas or topics. (Suggested: habitat, appearance, and behavior.) You might write general classifications on the chalkboard and show them how specific details fit under those headings.

3. Help them to complete an outline of the information they have compiled. Give each child a blank outline duplicated from the sheet in this unit.

OUTLINE FORM

_____

Topic

I. _____

   A. _____

   B. _____

   C. _____

II. _____

   A. _____

   B. _____

   C. _____

III. _____

   A. _____

   B. _____

   C. _____

SESSION FOUR

Materials
Lined paper, pencils, crayons and markers, staplers.

Activity
1. The students will write their reports.

2. When they have finished writing they should edit their work. Have them check the content for correct spelling, capitalization, and punctuation.

3. They may then staple their completed reports inside their folders.

4. They may decorate the fronts of their folders to correlate with the content of their reports. They may also write titles on their folders.
   (If they do not have time for this, it may be completed later at their desks when other assignments are completed.)

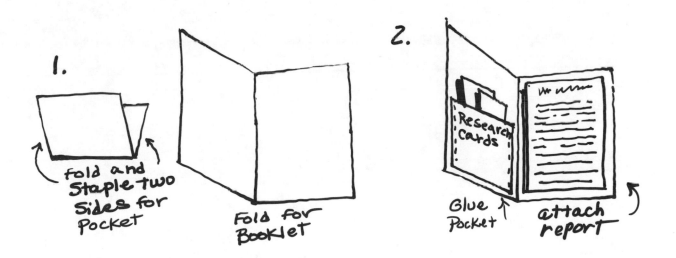

1. Fold and staple two sides for pocket
   Fold for booklet

2. Glue pocket — Research Cards — attach report

SESSION FIVE (Teacher Task Sheet)

This session includes a student task sheet and will be used to familiarize students with the Day's End Areas sign-up sheet, to give instruction as to where the areas are and how they are arranged, and to give students practice working individually in small groups. The children must learn to stay in the areas for the designated time. You float to guide, supervise, and discuss the topic on which they are working.

Materials

Sign-up sheet

Activity

1. Explain the purpose of the sign-up sheet that they will be using for each unit and have them sign up for the areas in which they will work (they will all be working on the same task for this unit).

2. Have the students pick up their task sheets and any needed materials, go to the proper areas, and complete their work independently.

SESSION FIVE (Student Task Sheet)

Materials
Scissors, black crayons or markers, glue, giraffe pattern sheets.

Activity
1. Color the spots black on the giraffe's body and legs.

2. Cut out the giraffe's body. You may need to reinforce the neck by gluing a strip of scrap paper on the back side.

3. Cut slits where indicated on the body.

4. Fold the leg pattern sheet in half lengthwise.

5. Form the folded sheet into a tube shape and slip one end inside the other end (see illustration).

6. Set the body in place on the leg section by slipping the slits in the body over the top of the tube.

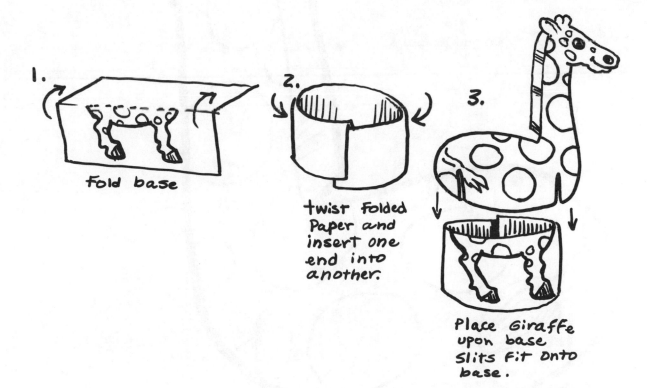

1. Fold base

2. twist folded paper and insert one end into another.

3. Place Giraffe upon base slits fit onto base.

Cut
Slit

Cut
Slit

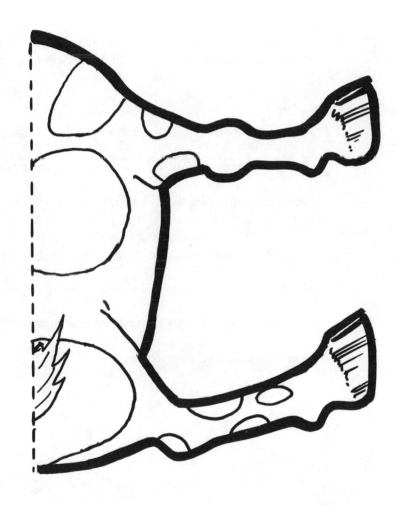

Name _____

INDIVIDUAL RESEARCH REPORT

Now that you have completed a research report with your teacher's help, you are ready to do one independently. Your subject will be *Hobbies*. Hobbies are such activities as sports, stamp collecting, photography, and many more.

Materials

Sheet of large construction paper, sheet of construction paper, stapler, glue, research card sheets, pencil, scissors, blank outline, lined paper, crayons and/or markers.

Activity

1. As you did before, make another research folder.

2. Choose a hobby about which you are interested in learning more.

3. Research from at least three media sources to learn about the topic. Use research cards on which to record the information that you discover.

4. Place the completed cards in the pocket in your folder.

5. Make an outline of the information that you gathered.

6. Write your report, edit it, and staple it into your folder.

7. Decorate and title your folder.

Animals

NOTES TO THE TEACHER

OBJECTIVES

To familiarize students with the habitats of various animals and the regions in which they live.

To help students become aware of the need for preserving animal species.

To help children learn to use facts creatively in writing.

MATERIALS

Scissors, glue, staplers, pencils, clay, clay modeling tools (popsicle sticks, pencils, tableware, sharpened dowels), gray and green construction paper, large (12" x 18") blue construction paper, white drawing paper, plastic or foil plates, crayons and markers, scratch paper.

TOPIC OF THE WEEK

This introductory activity is to be used with the class as a whole as an introduction to the unit. To allow the students time to read and gather information, it should be used a day or more before they go to Day's End Areas.

DAY'S END AREAS

Paper Crafts—Media Report Holder

The children will cut out and assemble paper beaver lodges. They will cut out paper logs. As they study media materials, they will cut off sections of the logs and keep the logs in the beaver lodge pockets.

Research Question Form

The children will develop questions that they would like to have answered about specific animals that they choose and will research to answer those and two printed questions.

Research and Writing—Pocket Riddles

On printed forms, the children will write riddles about animals, draw the animals, and make and decorate pockets to depict the regions in which the animals live.

(Prior to this activity, you need to discuss riddle writing with the children. The most general fact is given first followed by several other general facts. The best clue is given last in a riddle. You might also discuss what a region is and how it affects the animal life that is found there.

To motivate the children to do more riddles, you might tell them they will have an opportunity to share their riddles with others at the end of the unit.)

Poetry—An Animal Poem

The children will choose, copy, and illustrate favorite poems.

Language Arts—A Tangled Tale

The children must supply words to fill the blanks in a story. The words must be particular parts of speech which a leader will dictate. They will write the words they have chosen in the blanks of a story to create individual and amusing tales.

Clay Modeling—Extinct Animals

The children will learn the meaning of the word *extinct*, what causes animals to become extinct, and the names of several extinct animals. They will then create clay models of extinct animals.

(Discuss ways in which children can help in animal preservation as well as what is being done by others. It would be good to have a speaker come in, if possible.)

Creative Art—Animal Homes

The children will learn about various animals' homes. They will each create an artistic animal's home.

CULMINATING ACTIVITY

This is a perfect time for the children to share the riddles they wrote. They might also share some of their stories.

Name _____

TOPIC OF THE WEEK

Use the dictionary to find the meaning of the word *animal*. Write it below. _____

_____

_____

_____

What words do you associate with the word *animal*?

_____ _____

_____ _____

_____ _____

_____ _____

_____ _____

_____ _____

Make a list of any articles or stories about animals that are available to you from any media source (books, magazines, filmstrips, computer disks, tapes).

_____

_____

_____

_____

_____

_____

_____

_____

DAY'S END AREAS

PAPER CRAFTS

Materials
Scissors, glue or stapler, lodge pattern, pencil, crayons or markers, beaver pattern.

Activity

1. Cut out the beaver lodge.

2. Fold the lodge together on the dotted line. Glue or staple the side edges together.

3. Cut out and color the log.

4. Choose titles from the list of media materials that you made on the "Topic of the Week" sheet. Read, view, or listen to the material. When you have read a given number of pages (your teacher will tell you the number), cut off one curved log section. For material that you listen to or view, cut off one section for each fifteen minutes that you study. Keep the log in the lodge. On the back of the lodge, record each title that you study.

5. When you have cut off all the log sections, you may make Binky Beaver. Cut out the beaver, fold on the dotted line in the center, and glue the body together. Fold the feet and tail upward on the dotted lines, and Binky will stand alone.

BEAVER LODGE

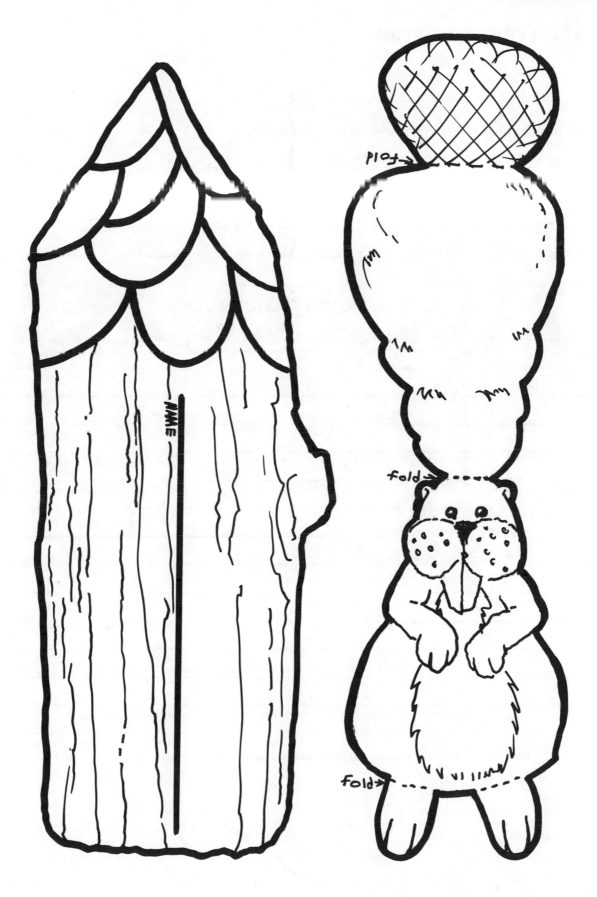

RESEARCH QUESTION FORM

ANIMAL _____   RESEARCHER _____

Questions that I would like to have answered by the research:

1. Where does the animal spend most of its time? _____

2. What does the animal eat? _____

3. _____

4. _____

5. _____

ANSWERS TO RESEARCH QUESTIONS

1. _____
    _____
    _____

2. _____
    _____
    _____

3. _____
    _____
    _____

4. _____
    _____

5. _____
    _____
    _____

On the back of this sheet, write a true or an imaginary story about the animal you have studied.

Name _____

RESEARCH AND WRITING

A riddle is a puzzling question or statement. Most people enjoy guessing answers to riddles.

Materials

Riddle card(s), crayons or markers, scissors, pocket pattern sheet(s), pencil, glue.

Activity

1. Learn about an animal of your choice. Write a riddle on the lines of a pocket riddle card.

2. On the bottom of the card, draw a picture that gives the answer (the animal your riddle is about). Cut out the card.

3. Cut out a pocket. Fold on the dotted lines. Glue the tabs on the sides.

4. Decorate the pocket to show the details of the region in which the animal lives (Example: a snow scene for a polar bear in the Arctic region).

5. Place the card in the pocket so the answer (picture) is hidden.

6. Do as many riddles and pockets as you like and have time to do.

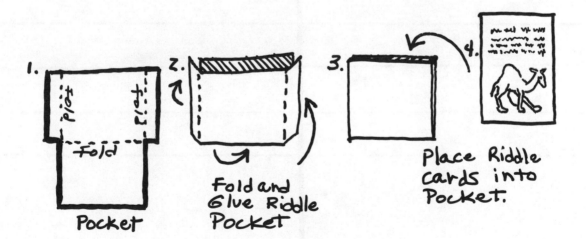

RIDDLE CARDS

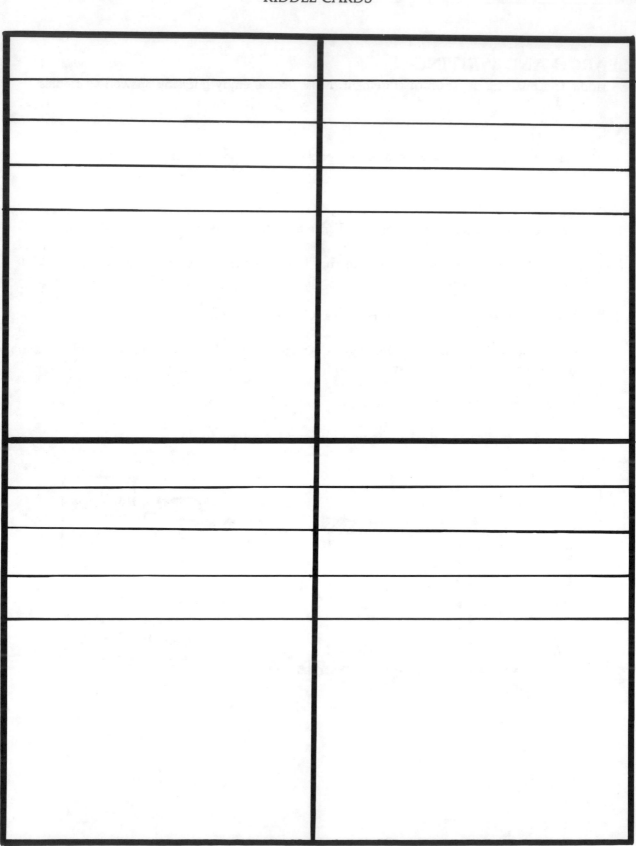

POCKET PATTERN

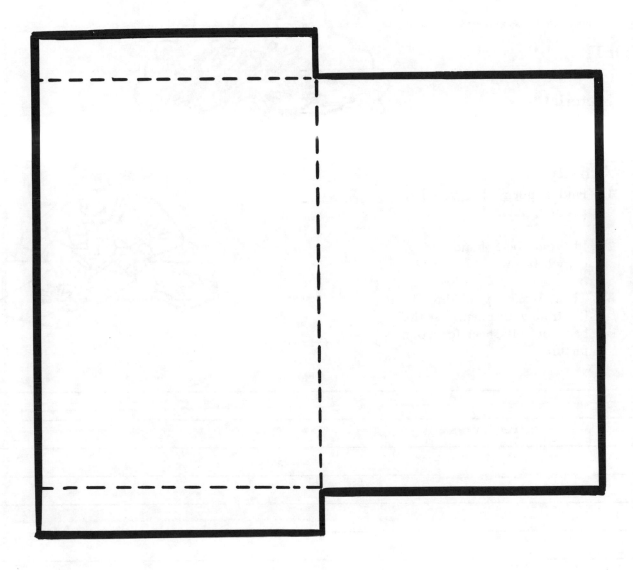

Name _____

POETRY

Materials
Pencil, crayons and/or markers.

Activity

1. Find a poem that you like about an animal.

2. In your best handwriting, copy it below.

3. Then make a picture to illustrate your poem. Use the back of this sheet for your picture.

_____

_____

_____

_____

_____

_____

_____

_____

_____

_____

_____

_____

_____

_____

_____

Name _____

LANGUAGE ARTS

Materials
Pencil, scratch paper.

Activity

1. In your group at the Day's End Area, choose a leader. Do not look at the story yet.

2. On a piece of scratch paper, write the words the leader tells you to write. (Leader: Read the words called for under the blanks in the Tangled Tale.)

3. Now write in order in the blanks in the story the words you have chosen.

4. Share your story with your group and/or class.

5. On the back of this sheet, write your own tangled tale about an animal.

ALL ABOUT SWAMPS
(Tangled Tale)

A swamp is a _____ that is always _____. Springs may feed the
             noun   adjective

low places or water may simply _____ there. There is no way for the water to _____
                                  verb   verb

away, so the land always stays _____.
                                        adjective

Many _____ such as alligators, _____, frogs,
               plural noun   name of a creature, plural

muskrats, and _____ may be found in a _____. Many kinds of birds also
                   a creature, plural   noun

_____ their homes there.
   verb

There are many kinds of plants such as water _____ and mosses. Trees
                                             name of a flower, plural

such as cyprus and _____ grow in _____. Some _____ have
                plural noun   plural noun   plural noun

many fish in them, too.

The United States has several _____ swamps such as the Everglades in Florida and
                               adjective

Okefenokee in Georgia and Florida. You might like to _____ one of these _____.
                                           verb   adverb

Draw a picture about your tale below.

Name _____

CLAY MODELING
Use the dictionary to learn the meaning of the word *extinct*. Write it below.

_____

_____

_____

Use an encyclopedia to find out and write two things that may cause animals to become extinct.

_____

_____

Name at least four animals that have become extinct.

_____   _____

_____   _____

_____   _____

Materials
Plastic or foil plates, clay, clay modeling tools (pencil, popsicle sticks, tableware, sharpened dowels), pencil.

Activity
1. Choose one extinct animal that you would like to make. Use books, articles, encyclopedias, or other media sources to learn about the animal.

2. On a plastic or foil plate, make a clay model of the animal you have chosen. Make it look as much like the animal as you can.

Name _____

CREATIVE ART

Animals live in many different kinds of places. Some birds live in trees. Bats live in caves. Work with your friends and think of all the places that you can in which animals live. Make a list on the back of this page. Then make a swamp, a cave, or some other animal home about which you have studied.

CAVE

Materials

Gray construction paper, white drawing paper, scissors, glue, pencil, crayons or markers.

Activity

1. From any media source, gather information about caves and the animals that live in them.

2. Use one sheet of gray construction paper or a sheet of white drawing paper that you color as you wish for the base of your cave.

3. Fold ½" tabs on the short ends of another sheet of construction paper. Use gray or color white paper as you wish.

4. Hold this sheet, tabs down, in a nice arch and mark on the bottom sheet where the glue lines will be.

5. Draw and color animals that you would find in caves. Cut them out, leaving ½" tabs on the bottoms. You may use those given on the pattern sheet, or you may draw your own. Be sure to add at least three items that you have created yourself.

6. Fold and glue the tabs on the inside top and on the bottom of your cave. You may add other formations such as stalagmites and stalactites to your cave. Remember that stalactites must "hang on tight" to the top of a cave and stalagmites form on the floor of a cave.

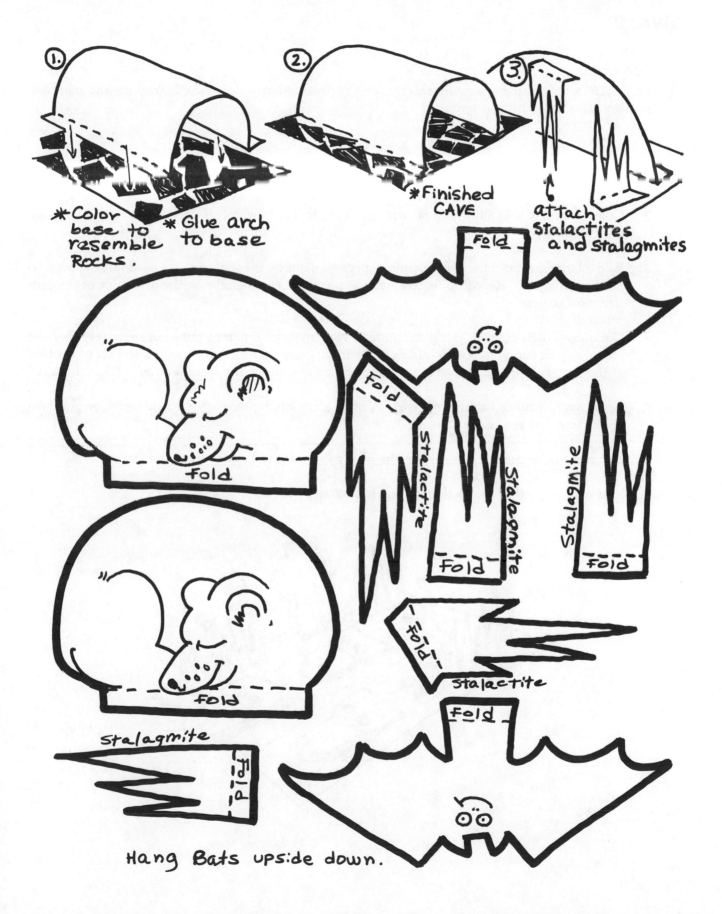

1.
*Color base to resemble Rocks.
*Glue arch to base

2.
*Finished CAVE

3.
attach stalactites and stalagmites

Fold

fold

fold

Fold

Stalactite

Stalagmite

Stalagmite

Fold

Fold

Fold

Stalactite

Fold

Stalagmite

Fold

Fold

Hang Bats upside down.

SWAMP

Materials

Large (12″ x 18″) blue construction paper, green construction paper, pencil, crayons and markers, scissors, glue, alligator pattern(s).

Activity

1. From any media source, gather information about swamps and the animals that live in them.

2. Color as many alligators as you want to have in your swamp. Glue the parts together (see illustration).

3. Fold a large sheet of blue construction paper and cut it on the fold to make a slit large enough to insert an alligator. Repeat for each animal you make. Glue the tabs on the underside of the construction paper.

4. Cut out as many trees as you plan to use in your swamp. You may cut your own trees, bushes, etc. in any design you like by folding and cutting green paper. Leave uncut a section of the fold at the top. Fold the tabs. Cut slits as you did before, insert the trees, and glue them in place.

5. Grass may be made in the same way. Always leave some places on the fold uncut or glue two pieces together above the tabs.

6. Arrange the animals and plants on the blue paper so you have a pretty swamp.

7. You may add other things that belong in a swamp, if you wish.

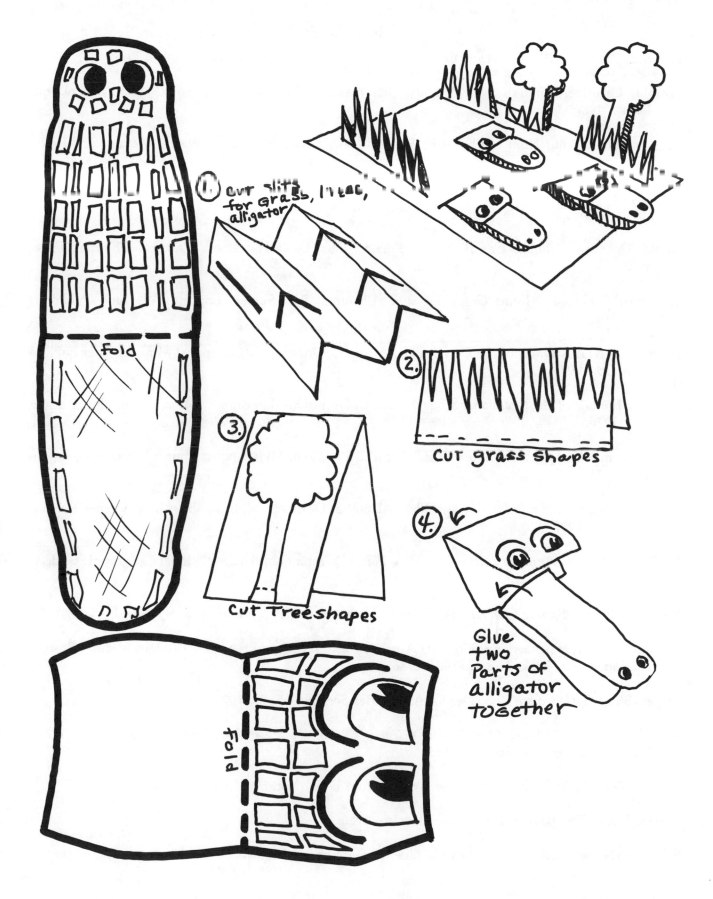

1. Cut slits for grass, trees, alligator

2. Cut grass shapes

3. Cut Treeshapes

Fold

Fold

4. Glue two Parts of alligator together

BIBLIOGRAPHY

Armour, Richard. *Odd Old Animals*. Illus. Paul Galdone. New York: McGraw-Hill Book Co., 1986.

Arnold, Caroline. *Animals That Migrate*. Illus. Michele Zylman. Minneapolis, Minn.: Carolrhoda Books, 1982.

_____. *Pets without Homes*. Photos by Richard Hewett. Boston: Clarion Books, Ticknor and Fields, 1983.

Bellville, Rod, and Cheryl Walsh Bellville. *Large Animal Veterinarians*. Minneapolis, Minn.: Carolrhoda Books, Inc., 1983.

Chald, Dorothy. *Animals Can Be Special Friends*. Illus. Lydia Halverson. Chicago: Childrens Press, 1985.

Cloudsley-Thompson, John. *Crocodiles and Alligators*. East Sussex, England: Wayland Publishers Ltd., 1980.

Johnson, Sylvia. *Animals of the Desert*. Illus. Alcuin C. Dornisch. Minneapolis, Minn.: Lerner Publications Co., 1976.

_____. *Animals of the Grasslands*. Illus. Alcuin C. Dornisch. Minneapolis, Minn.: Lerner Publications Co., 1976.

_____. *Animals of the Mountains*. Illus. Alcuin C. Dornisch. Minneapolis, Minn.: Lerner Publications Co., 1976.

_____. *Animals of the Polar Regions*. Illus. Alcuin C. Dornisch. Minneapolis, Minn.: Lerner Publications Co., 1976.

McCauley, Jane R. *Animals and Their Hiding Places*. Washington, D.C.: National Geographic Society, 1986.

McGrath, Susan. *Saving Our Animal Friends*. Washington, D.C.: National Geographic Society, 1986.

Patent, Dorothy Hinshaw. *Buffalo: The American Bison Today*. Photos by William Muñoz. Boston: Clarion Books, Ticknor and Fields, 1986.

Rieger, Shay. *The Bronze Zoo*. New York: Charles Scribner's Sons, 1970.

Rinard, Judith E. *Helping Our Animal Friends*. Photos by Susan McElhinney. Washington, D.C.: National Geographic Society, 1985.

_____. *The World Beneath Your Feet*. Washington, D.C.: National Geographic Society, 1985.

Ryden, Hope. *The Beaver*. New York: Putnam, 1986.

Sabin, Francene. *Swamps and Marshes*. Illus. Barbara Flynn. Mahwah, N.J.: Troll Associates, 1985.

Birds

NOTES TO THE TEACHER

OBJECTIVES

To increase students' knowledge and appreciation of birds in the environment.

To increase students' knowledge of birds in the particular area in which they live.

MATERIALS

Scissors, glue or staples, crayons and markers, 3" x 5" index cards, bird stickers (optional), clay, clay modeling tools (popsicle sticks, pencils, tableware, sharpened dowels), plastic or foil plates, scratch paper, blue and white construction paper.

TOPIC OF THE WEEK

This introductory activity is to be used with the class as a whole as an introduction to the unit. To allow the students time to read and gather information, it should be used a day or more before they go to Day's End Areas.

DAY'S END AREAS

Paper Crafts—Media Report Holder

The children will cut out, assemble, and decorate a pocket in the form of a birdhouse. It will be used to store completed media report forms.

Media Report Form

On these forms, the children will record information about the media materials that they have studied.

Research and Writing—Birds to Color

The children will research to discover the proper colors for the birds shown on picture cards. They will color the birds correctly and record other facts they have learned about the birds.

There is a blank card sheet on which the children may draw and color birds of their choice in addition to those pictured in the unit.

Clay—A Bird Model

The children will each research a particular bird (or parts of more than one such as wings, bills, or feet) and then make a detailed clay model of that bird.

Language Arts—A Tangled Tale

The children must supply words that are given parts of speech which a leader will dictate. The words will then be written in the blanks of a story to create individual and amusing tales.

Art—Water Birds

The children will gather information about water birds, make paper replicas of the birds, and create scenes with the birds "swimming" on construction paper ponds.

Social Studies—Interviewing a Volunteer

Some of the children will volunteer to gather information about the National Audubon Society. Others will develop questions to be used for interviewing the volunteers.

Volunteer Worker's Contract

This form will be used by you and the students to plan their activities for gathering information in preparation for being interviewed about the National Audubon Society.

CULMINATING ACTIVITY

So the class can share information, set up an interview panel with the interviewers using the questions they developed to query the volunteers who gathered information about the National Audubon Society.

Having a speaker from the National Audubon Society come in and talk to the children would also be a nice culminating activity, if this possibility exists in your area.

Name _____

TOPIC OF THE WEEK

Use the dictionary to find the meaning of the word *bird*. Write the meaning on the lines below.

_____

_____

_____

What words do you associate with the word *bird*?

_____ _____

_____ _____

_____ _____

_____ _____

_____ _____

_____ _____

Make a list of any articles or stories about the topic that are available to you from any media source (books, magazines, filmstrips, computer disks, tapes).

_____

_____

_____

_____

_____

_____

_____

_____

_____

_____

_____

Name _____

DAY'S END AREAS

PAPER CRAFTS

Materials
Scissors, glue or staples, crayons or markers, an approximately 3" x 5" card, bird sticker (optional).

Activity

1. Cut out the birdhouse pattern. Cut out the hole.

2. Fold the birdhouse together on the dotted line.

3. Glue or staple the side edges together.

4. Use crayons or markers to decorate your birdhouse.

5. Slip a card into the pocket and mark the position of the hole. Draw a bird picture or mount a sticker in this space. Slip the card into the pocket so that the bird picture appears in the hole.

6. Choose titles from the media materials list that you made on the "Topic of the Week" sheet. Read, view, or listen to the materials. Complete a media report card for each title that you study. Place the cards in your birdhouse.

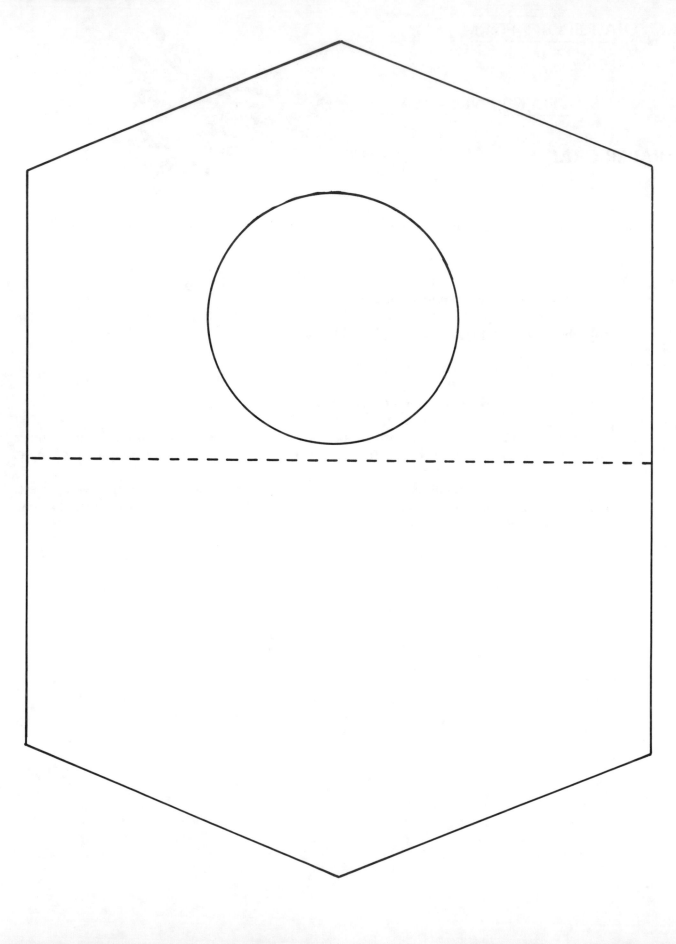

MEDIA REPORT FORM

For each item you read or hear, cut out and complete a report card. When you have finished your media report holder, place the completed cards in the holder. Use the back of the card for assignments.

My name is _____

Title of Book or Media Materials

Name of Author

Name of Illustrator

What did you discover in the material that was new to you?

My name is _____

Title of Book or Media Materials

Name of Author

Name of Illustrator

Comments:

My name is _____

Title of Book or Media Materials

Name of Author

Name of Illustrator

Write a paragraph or draw a picture of the most interesting part of what you studied.

My name is _____

Title of Book or Media Materials

Name of Author

Name of Illustrator

Briefly tell about what you studied.

Name _____

RESEARCH AND WRITING

Materials
Pencil, crayons or markers, two sheets of bird cards, scissors.

Activity

1. Use encyclopedias, bird books, magazines or other media sources to learn about these birds.

2. On the backs of the cards, write what you have learned about each bird.

3. Then color each bird correctly.

4. If you want to draw and color some other birds that you choose, use a blank card sheet.

5. Cut the cards apart on the lines. Place the finished cards in your birdhouse with your media report forms.

Parrot

Hummingbird

Kingfisher

White Pelican

Canada goose

Common Loon

Puffin

Meadowlark

Name _____

CLAY MODELING

Materials

Clay of various colors, tools (popsicle stick, pencil, tableware, sharpened dowel), plastic or foil plate for a base.

Activity

1. Decide what you would like to model, an entire bird or parts of more than one (feet, wings, bills). Study (books, magazines, encyclopedias, or other media sources) to learn about the bird or birds. Notice detail (exactly what a thing looks like).

2. Make a clay model or models of the bird or bird parts you have chosen to make. Show as much detail as you can. Make each tiny part as much like the real bird as you can.

3. In the space below, draw a sketch of your clay creation.

Name _____

LANGUAGE ARTS

Materials
Pencil, scratch paper.

Activity

1. In your group at the Day's End Area, choose a leader. Do not look at the story below yet.

2. On a piece of scratch paper, write the words the leader tells you to write. (Leader: Read the words called for under the blanks in the Tangled Tale.)

3. Now write in order in the blanks in the story the words you have chosen.

4. Share your story with your group and/or class.

BOBBIN, THE ROBIN
(Tangled Tale)

Bobbin, a _____ robin, was busy hunting for her _____. Sunlight danced
          adjective   noun

through the tree _____ and _____ her back. All at once, she
         noun (plural)   verb ending in ed

_____ her head and listened with her sharp _____ ears. What she heard
  verb ending in ed   adjective

was a loud, "Tee hee, tee hee, tee hee."

"Are you _____ at me?"
       verb ending in ing

"Tee hee. I might be."

"Who are you? Where are you?"

"I'm here. Can't you see me?"

"Why are you _____ at me?"
         verb ending in ing

"Tee hee. You're silly!"

"I am not. Can't you see I'm building my _____ nest?"
                   adjective

"That's silly. You work too hard."

"It is not! Are you a _____?"
        name of a living creature

"Guess. Tee hee. Tee hee."

"How can I guess? I can only hear you."

"Tell me what you know about me."

"I know you're noisy," Robin answered.

"Yes. What else?"

"Do you have a _____?"
part of a living creature

"Yes."

"Do you have a _____?"
part of a living creature

"No."

"You must be _____."
adjective to describe a creature

"No, I'm not!"

"Do you have two _____?"
part of a creature (plural)

"Yes, I do."

"Do you have four _____?"
part of a creature (plural)

"No, I don't have any. I am _____ and _____."
a color   a color

"Where do you live? I live in a nest."

"I know where you live. Tee hee. I live in a _____. And my
a creature's home

_____ is _____. I like _____
part of a creature   adjective to describe part of a creature   a food

best of all. Tee hee!"

Bobbin stopped pecking and scratching and just looked in the direction of the noise. She could barely chirp, "Well, I'll just call you a Tee Hee. And you said I was silly!"

List on a piece of paper the features your Tee Hee has: two feet, hair, no tail, etc. Now, on the back of this sheet, draw your Tee Hee.

CREATIVE ART

Materials

Pencil, blue construction paper, white construction paper, index cards, crayons or markers, scissors.

Activity

1. Gather information from any media sources about three or more water birds.

2. Draw a small picture of each bird you have chosen and color it correctly. Cut out the pictures. Number each bird on the back.

3. Fold a piece of blue construction paper accordian style (see illustration). Slit across the tops of three folds on one long side of the folded paper. Make other slits in the tops of the folds, one for each bird you have made. Arrange the slits so that your birds will look nice "swimming" on the "pond." Slip the birds into the slits.

4. Number index cards on the top lines as you numbered the birds you made. On card #1, write a paragraph about bird #1. Do this for each bird. Place the cards across the three slits you made at the back of the "pond."

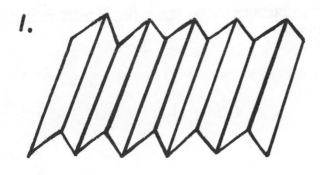

Name _____

SOCIAL STUDIES

Materials
Pencil, Volunteer Workers Contract

Activity

1. Decide if you want to be a volunteer (one who does extra work to help others learn) or an interviewer. Sign up, so that about half the group is participating in each part of the activity.

2. If you decide to volunteer, use a Volunteer Worker's Contract to plan your activity. Find out all that you can about the National Audubon Society. Use reference books and the library. Talk to your parents and/or someone who is a member of the society. Use the back of this sheet to record all the information that you find.

3. An interviewer is one who asks questions of someone who knows about an event or is an expert in some field. An interviewer needs to know such things as: what happened, what a thing is, who is involved, where it is, why it happened or why it exists, how it will help people, and similar facts. Write questions below that, as an interviewer, you would like to know about the National Audubon Society, its purpose, and its activities.

VOLUNTEER WORKER'S CONTRACT

Materials
Pencil

Name of Project _____

Purpose of Project _____

_____

_____

Materials Needed: _____

_____

Information Gathered About Topic (Use back of sheet, if more space is needed.)

_____

_____

_____

_____

_____

_____

_____

_____

_____

How I Plan To Use This Information

_____

_____

_____

_____

_____

_____

_____

Date Started _____

Date To Complete _____

Date Completed _____

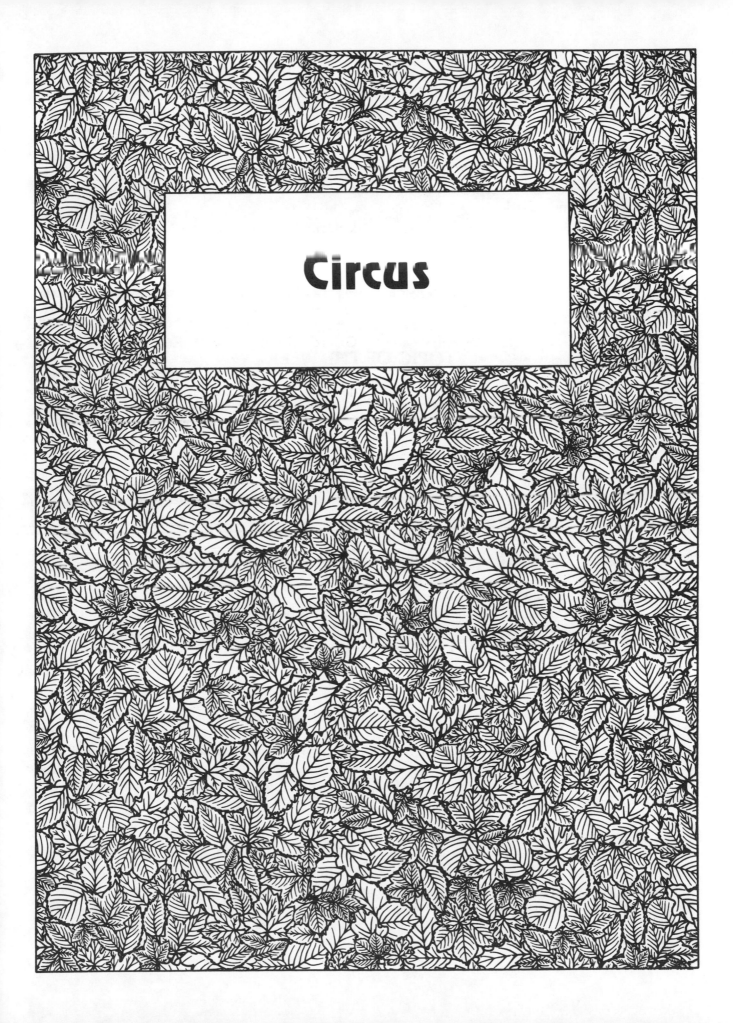

Circus

OBJECTIVES

To familiarize students with the history of some famous circuses.

To help students experience the excitement of the circus and to use this excitement in writing and in choosing reading material.

MATERIALS

Pencils, scissors, glue, crayons and markers, straws (or pipe cleaners), string or yarn, tape (optional), clay, plastic or foil plates, other materials to complete a clay scene (straws, paper, twigs, etc.), scrap paper.

TOPIC OF THE WEEK

This introductory activity is to be used with the class as a whole as an introduction to the unit. To allow the students time to read and gather information, it should be used a day or more before they go to Day's End Areas.

DAY'S END AREAS

Paper Crafts—Media Report Holder and Forms

The children will cut out and assemble elephant pockets in which to store completed media report forms.

(The elephant should be duplicated on pink paper.)

The students will record on peanut-shaped forms information about the media materials they have studied. They will cut out the forms and store them in the elephant pockets.

(Duplicate the peanut forms on light brown paper.)

Art—Circus Performers

The children will each cut out and assemble three circus performers: a monkey on a trapeze, a trapeze artist, and a clown.

(Duplicate the monkey on light brown paper. Duplicate extra sheets. For young children, prepare the straws ahead of time by sucking pieces of string through the straws. Tie the ends together and slip the knots inside of the straws to form trapezes. Older children will enjoy it and can do this safely themselves.)

Language Arts—A Tangled Tale

The children must supply words that are given parts of speech which a leader will dictate. The words will then be written in the blanks of a story to create individual and amusing tales.

(At a later time, you might like to have the children use the tale as a cloze procedure exercise and fill in the blanks with words that make sense.)

Writing—My Clown Story
The children will color pictures and write stories based on the pictures.

Research—Famous Circuses
The children will use various media sources to learn about two famous circuses.

Clay—A Circus Scene
The children will each model a circus scene with clay and other materials.
(Provide a sign-up sheet so that the scenes the children make are varied.)

CULMINATING ACTIVITY
Let the children be clowns for a day. Let them dress as clowns and present skits, singly or as groups. Encourage them to vary their costumes. If possible, provide a prize for the best or most unusual costume.

TOPIC OF THE WEEK

Find the word *circus* in a dictionary and write its meaning below.

_____

_____

_____

_____

What words do you associate with the word *circus*?

_____   _____

_____   _____

_____   _____

_____   _____

_____   _____

Make a list of any articles or stories about the topic that are available to you from any media source (books, magazines, filmstrips, computer disks, tapes).

_____

_____

_____

_____

_____

_____

_____

_____

_____

_____

_____

Name _____

DAY'S END AREAS

PAPER CRAFTS

Materials
Elephant pattern, scissors, glue, crayons, or markers.

Activity

1. Cut out the elephant.

2. Cut out the pocket and place it behind the elephant's trunk (see illustration). Glue the pocket to the trunk along the curved edge.

3. Use your elephant pocket for storing completed media report forms.

Pocket Piece

Glue this piece to back of elephant's trunk.

Glue

Glue

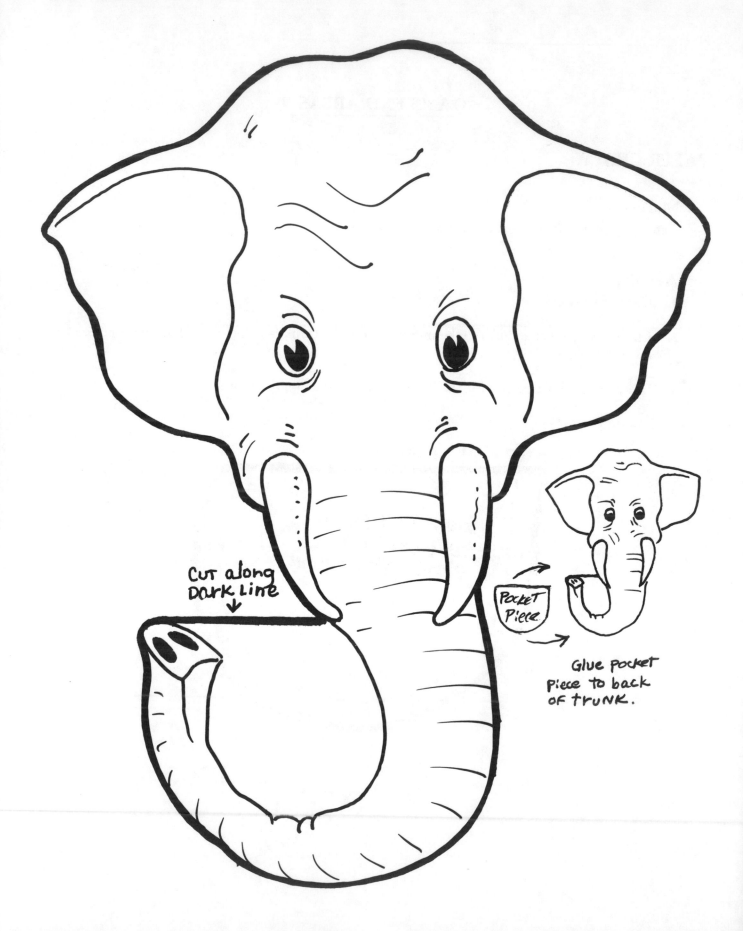

Cut along
Dark Line

POCKET
Piece

Glue pocket
piece to back
of TRUNK.

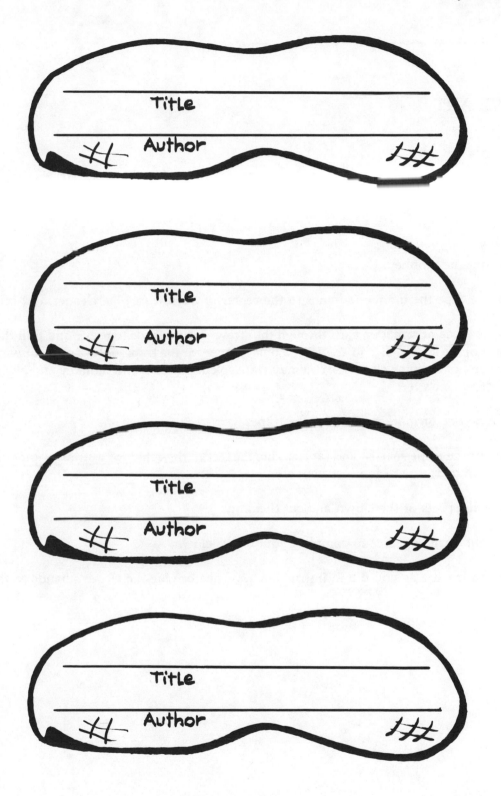

Name _____

CREATIVE ART

Materials
Trapeze artist, monkey, and clown patterns, crayons or markers, scissors, straws (or pipe cleaners), string or yarn, glue or tape.

Activity

1. Cut out the monkey.

2. Glue or tape the monkey's hands to the center of a straw or pipe cleaner.

3. Suck a piece of string or yarn through the straw. Tie the ends together and pull the knot to the inside of the straw. (If you are using a pipe cleaner for the trapeze, tie a piece of yarn or string to each end of the pipe cleaner.) You may want to cut out a second monkey and glue the hands to the other one's feet.

4. Use crayons or markers to color the trapeze artist.

5. Cut out the trapeze artist and tape or glue the feet to the center of a straw or pipe cleaner. Form the trapeze as you did in instruction #3.

6. Color the parts of the clown and cut them out.

7. Glue the parts together to complete your circus clown.

8. Make a trapeze as you did in instruction #3. Tape or glue the clown's hands to the trapeze.

Glue

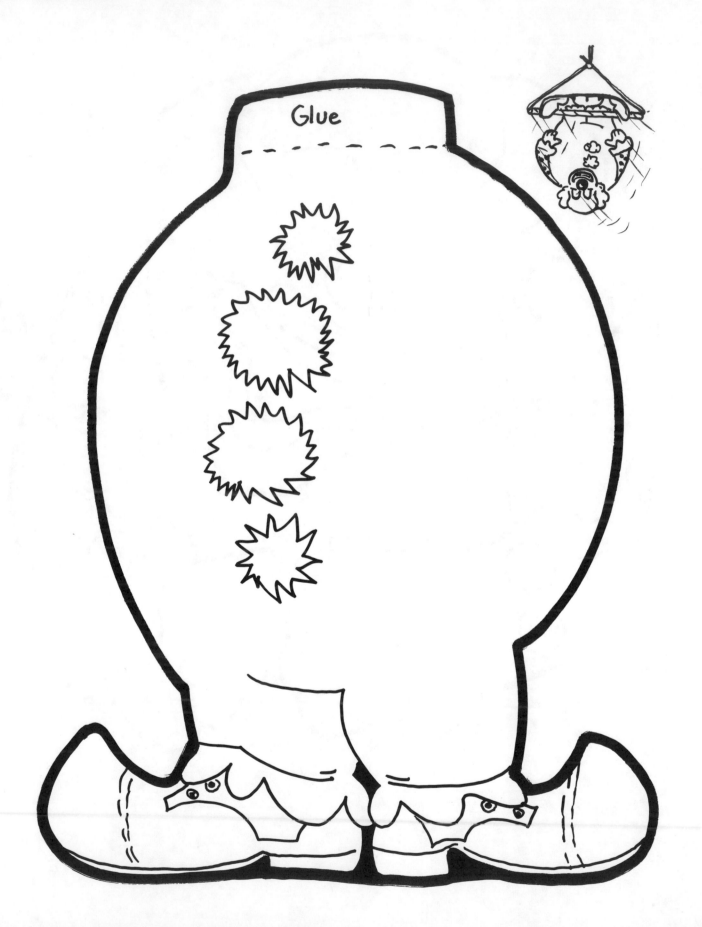

Glue

Name _____

LANGUAGE ARTS

Materials
Pencil, scratch paper.

Activity

1. In your group at the Day's End Area, choose a leader. Do not look at the story below yet.

2. On a piece of scratch paper, write the words that the leader tells you to write. (Leader: Read the words that are called for under the blanks in the Tangled Tale.) Use the same girl's name throughout. Use the same name for Boy 1 each time, for Boy 2, etc. You will use four different boys' names.

3. Now write in order in the blanks in the story the words that you have chosen.

4. Share your story with your group and/or class.

AN AERIAL RESCUE
(Tangled Tale)

On a very hot day _____ worried that her _____
                  a girl in the room   part of the body, plural

would slip from _____'s after her aerial somersault. _____
                1. a boy in the room   1. boy in the room

swung far out on the trapeze. _____ swung out. They _____
                           girl in the room   verb ending in ed

in the air.

    Just then, she heard a laugh-like _____. To her horror, she saw _____,
                                      noun   2. a boy in the room

one of the twin monkeys, leap onto the upper rope of _____'s trapeze. Any tiny
                                             1. boy in the room

thing to upset their timing could cause a/an _____ fall. Would _____
                                    adjective   1. boy in the room

feel the tug and allow for it? There was _____, the other monkey, on the platform!
                                   3. a boy in the room

_____'s heart was _____ against her ribs. She was scared. She
    girl in the room   verb ending in ing

didn't leap on the first pass—or the second. Would _____ understand?
                                           1. boy in the room

The crowd cheered and _____ so _____ that her
    (verb ending in ed)   (adverb telling "how")

_____ hurt. _____ the ladder was another, very large monkey.
    (a part of the body)   (verb ending in ing)

Just then a furry _____ grabbed _____. The big monkey
                     (a part of the body)   (3. boy in room)

seemed to be falling. The crowd _____. Then, hanging off the platform by one
                                     (verb ending in ed)

_____, it reached toward the flying swing. _____ leaped and
    (a part of the body)   (2. boy in room)

_____ on the outstretched _____. The big monkey waved in
    (verb ending in ed)   (a part of the body)

space, looking as if a terrible _____ were certain.
                                     (noun)

On the next pass, _____ launched herself forward and up. She _____
                     (a girl in the room)   (verb ending in ed)

over twice in the air and caught _____'s _____. They
                                     (1. boy in the room)   (a part of the body, plural)

sailed gracefully to the platform and _____ at the crowd—but, the crowd was not
                                          (verb ending in ed)

looking at them. They were _____ at an unmasked _____
                              (verb ending in ing)   (4. boy in the room)

the clown, _____ down the ladder with two small monkeys in one _____.
              (verb ending in ing)   (a part of the body)

And climbing to the top of the bleachers was usually higher than _____
                                                                     (4. boy in the room)

would ever climb!

Name _____

CREATIVE WRITING

Materials
Pencil, crayons or markers.

Activity

1. Color the picture below.

2. Then write a story about the picture. The words in the Word Bank may help you. Use the lined sheet that is provided on which to complete your story.

circus	ring	frightening	show
clown	balloon	funny	stars
tricks	cannon	air	predict
laugh	light	future	animals

Page _____

_____
_____
_____
_____
_____
_____
_____
_____
_____
_____
_____
_____
_____
_____
_____
_____
_____
_____
_____
_____
_____
_____
_____
_____
_____
_____
_____
_____

EDITED: _____ (I checked for content, capitalization, and punctuation.)
      (X)

Name _____

RESEARCH

The Ringling Brothers' Circus and the Barnum and Bailey Circus were probably the most famous circuses in America. They eventually joined to become one circus and that circus is still in existence today, though it is under different ownership.

Materials

Pencil

Activity

Use books, encyclopedias, or other media sources to discover the following facts about these circuses.

The Ringling Brothers' Circus began as a wagon (traveling) show in _____.

It was bought by Barnum and Bailey in _____.

It joined with the Barnum and Bailey Circus in _____.

The Barnum and Bailey Circus began in _____.

Name and describe some characters from the Barnum and Bailey Circus.

_____

_____

_____

_____

_____

_____

_____

_____

_____

_____

_____ was the world's largest circus.

What was another name for the Barnum and Bailey Circus?

_____

Answer key on page 72.

Name _____

CLAY MODELING

Materials
Clay, other materials of your choice (straw, paper, twigs, etc.), foil or plastic plate.

Activity

1. Decide what circus scene you would like to model with clay. On a sheet that your teacher will provide, sign up to make that scene, if no one else has chosen the same scene.

2. In the space below, sketch the scene you plan to make.

3. Make your scene on a plate. You may use straws, paper, or other materials in addition to clay.

BIBLIOGRAPHY

Burnside, Irvine L. *The First American Circus Ever*. Illus. Sam Viviano. New York: Contemporary Perspectives, 1978.

Cone, Molly. *The Ringling Brothers*. Illus. James and Ruth McCrea. New York: Thomas Y. Crowell, 1971.

Fenten, D. X., and Barbara Fenten. *Behind the Circus Scene*. Mankato, Minn.: Crestwood House, Inc., 1980.

Harkonen, Helen B. *Circuses and Fairs in Art*. Minneapolis, Minn.: Lerner Publications, 1965.

Harmer, M. *The Circus*. Chicago: Childrens Press, 1981.

Kelly, Karin. *Careers with the Circus*. Photos by Milton J. Blumenfeld. Minneapolis, Minn.: Lerner Publications, 1975.

Klayer, Connie, and Joanna Kuhn. *Circus Time: How to Put on Your Own Show*. Illus. Carol Nicklaus. New York: Lothrop, Lee, and Shepard, 1979.

McGovern, Ann. *If You Lived with the Circus*. Illus. Ati Forberg. New York: Four Winds Press, 1972.

O'Connor, Vincent F. *In the Circus Ring*. Illus. Mike Jackson. Milwaukee, Wis.: MacDonald-Raintree, 1978.

O'Kelley, Mattie Lou. *Circus!* Boston/New York: The Atlantic Monthly Press, 1986.

Prelutsky, Jack. *Circus*. Illus. Arnold Lobel. New York: Macmillan Publishing Co., 1974.

Sobol, Harriet Langsam. *Clowns*. Photographs by Patricia Ogre. New York: Coward McCann and Geoghegan, Inc., 1982.

Stevenson, Augusta. *Wilbur and Orville Wright: Young Fliers*. Illus. Robert Doremus. New York: Aladdin Books, Macmillan Publishing Co., 1986.

West, Robin. *Paper Circus (How to Create Your Own Circus)*. Minneapolis, Minn.: Carolrhoda Books, Inc., 1983.

ANSWER KEY

RESEARCH

1884

1907

1919

1871

(Jenny Lind—a singer
Jumbo—large elephant
Tom Thumb—a midget
There may be others.)

The Ringling Brothers

The Greatest Show on Earth

Continents

NOTES TO THE TEACHER

OBJECTIVES

To help students become aware of the topography and the plant and animal life of the continents.
To increase students' map skills.

MATERIALS

Dictionaries, long sheets of white paper, glue, markers or crayons, colored pencils, gummed stars (optional), reference maps of the continents, paper (optional).

TOPIC OF THE WEEK

This introductory activity is to be used with the class as a whole as an introduction to the unit. To allow the students time to read and gather information, it should be used a day or more before they go to Day's End Areas.

DAY'S END AREAS

Map Literature

The children will find and color continents on maps as they study about them or enjoy stories with settings on particular continents.

(You may want to provide gummed stars for the children or simply let them draw stars on the "Topic of the Week" sheet.)

Art—A Picture Postcard

The children will research facts and things of interest about particular continents and will then illustrate picture postcards.

(Sheets approximately 36″ long by 6″ wide should be provided for the students. Shorter sheets can be glued together by overlapping one section on each of two sheets and gluing.)

You might want to show the children some examples of picture postcards before they begin this activity.

So that all continents are studied in depth, you may want to assign continents for certain students to research. Suggest that they might learn about products, places of interest, climate, clothing worn, and the culture (art, music, literature) of the continent.

Social Studies—Map Skills

The children will research facts about the seven continents and will label maps of the continents as instructed.

(Help the students find appropriate reference books. Children might be able to bring atlases or other reference maps from home. Travel agencies might be able to provide maps. You might want the children to make scrapbooks with pictures, text, and maps of Europe after they have completed the activity sheet about Europe, or they might write reports using research folders.)

CULMINATING ACTIVITY

The students may share their picture postcards and/or their in-depth reports about continents. Encourage them to stand and speak in loud voices as they share their cards and information. You might start by asking for volunteers and then calling on others. Encourage them to share the information with their parents, also.

Name _____

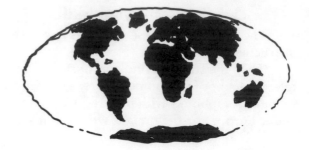

TOPIC OF THE WEEK

Use the dictionary to learn the meaning of the word
continent. Write it below.

_____

_____

_____

Using any media source, learn the names of the seven continents. Write them below. Place a star beside
the continent on which you live.

_____   _____

_____   _____

_____   _____

_____

Make a list of any articles about continents or stories with settings on continents other than your own
that are available to you from any media source (books, magazines, filmstrips, computer disks, tapes).

_____

_____

_____

_____

_____

_____

_____

_____

_____

_____

_____

DAY'S END AREAS

MAP LITERATURE

Materials
Pencil, crayons or colored pencils, gummed stars (optional)

Activity

1. Read, view, or listen to a title from the list that you made on the "Topic of the Week" sheet.

2. When you have studied about a continent or enjoyed a story with a setting on a particular continent, find and color that continent on the map below.

3. On the "Topic of the Week" sheet, place a star beside the title that you studied.

4. Try to finish coloring all the continents.

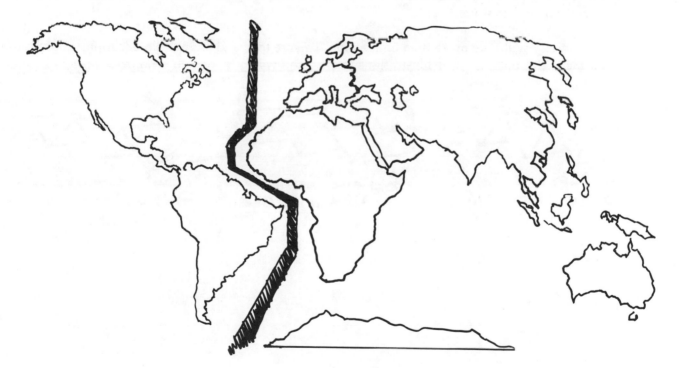

Color Australia red.
Color Europe yellow.
Color Antarctica blue.
Color South America pink.

Color Asia purple.
Color North America green.
Color Africa orange.

Name _____

CREATIVE ART

Materials
Long sheet of white paper, glue, markers and crayons, pencil.

Activity

1. Fan-fold a long sheet of white paper so that you have about six or seven sections.

2. Fold one end section in half and glue it together. Then cut off the corners to form a flap (see illustration).

3. Choose a continent to which you would like to take an imaginary trip. It may be your own. Study and find out all that you can about that continent.

4. Now create a picture postcard to give to a family member. Your postcard should show things of interest on that continent.

5. This activity will take more than one session. Be sure to spend enough time learning about the continent and making your illustrations so that you will be proud to send your postcard.

1. fold Paper into seven sections

2. fold end Section in half and Glue.

3. cut corners of folded end section to create a flap

Name _____

SOCIAL STUDIES

AFRICA

Materials
Dictionary, reference map, pencil, crayons or colored pencils, outline map sheet, paper (optional).

Activity
1. Complete the following tasks:
   a. Write the definition of the word *sea*.

   _____

   b. On the outline map, locate and label the Red Sea and the Mediterranean Sea.
   c. Write the definition of the word *canal*.

   _____

   d. On the outline map, label the Suez Canal.
   e. Write the definition of the word *equator*.

   _____

   f. On the outline map, draw and label the equator.
   g. Locate and label the following places: North Atlantic Ocean, South Atlantic Ocean, Indian Ocean, Canary Islands, Madeira Islands, Island of Madagascar, Nile River, Mt. Kilimanjaro, Sahara Desert.
   h. In the boxes below, draw one animal and one plant that can be found on the continent of Africa.

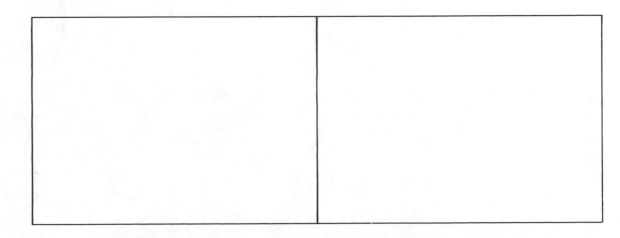

2. On the back of this sheet or on another sheet of paper, write any other interesting facts that you have learned about Africa. You may also draw illustrations of other plants and animals of Africa.

AFRICA

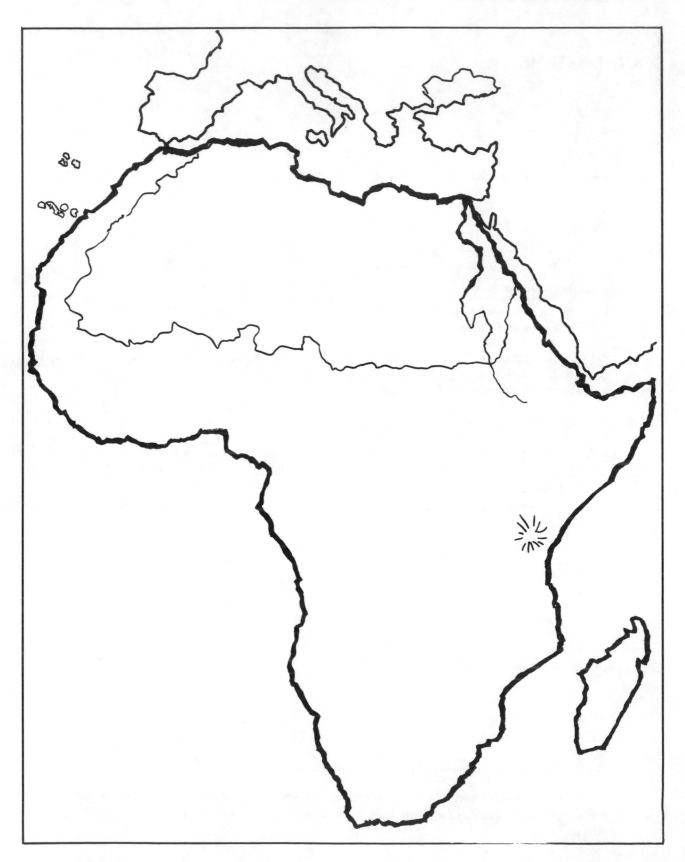

Name _____

ANTARCTICA

Materials
Pencil, dictionary, reference map, outline map sheet, crayons or markers, paper (optional).

Activity

1. Antarctica is a continent at the bottom of the earth. On your outline map, label Wilkes Land, Queen Maud Land, Coats Land, Marie Byrd Land, Victoria Land, and Enderby Land.

2. The term "South Pole" is used for several invisible surface points in the Antarctic region. The best known pole is the geographic pole. Label it on the outline map. Find and label the south magnetic pole.

3. Label the Antarctic Peninsula on the outline map.

4. The Antarctic Circle is an imaginary line that forms the northern boundary of Antarctica. Find and label this circle on the map.

5. A latitude line is an imaginary line measured in degrees that shows the distance north or south of the equator. Label the latitude lines on your map.

6. Use the dictionary or encyclopedia and fill in the blanks below.

   a. An icecap is _____

   b. An iceberg is _____

   c. An explorer is _____

7. On the back of this sheet, draw one animal and one plant that can be found on the continent of Antarctica.

8. On the back of this sheet or on another sheet of paper, write any other interesting facts that you have learned about Antarctica. You may also draw illustrations of other plants and animals of Antarctica, if you wish.

9. You might enjoy discovering information about one of the following explorers of Antarctica: Robert F. Scott, Sir Ernest H. Shackleton, Sir James C. Ross, Charles Wilkes, Roald Amundsen, or Richard E. Byrd. Prepare a written or oral report about the explorer that you choose to research.

ANTARCTICA

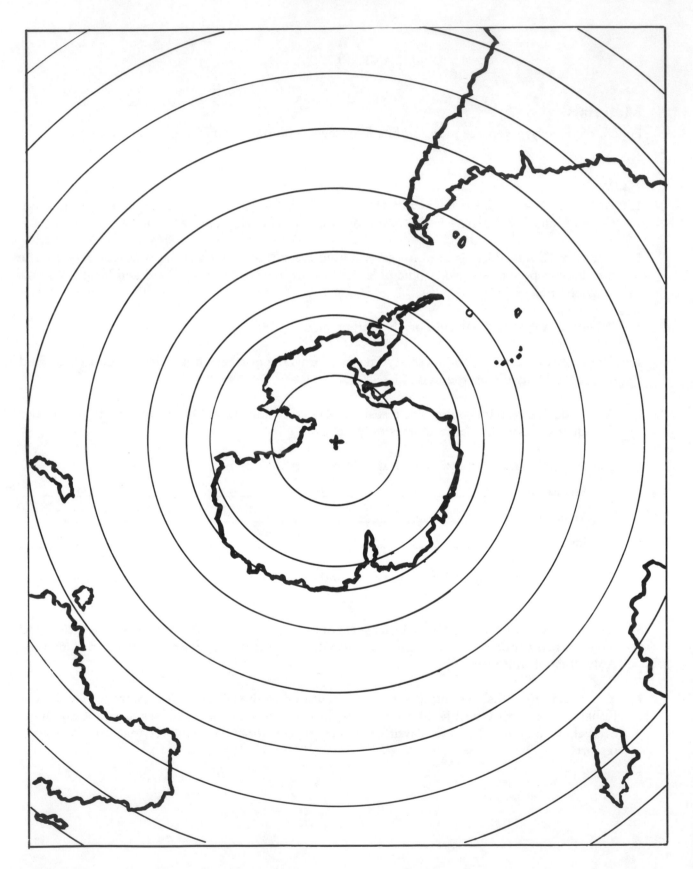

Name _____

ASIA

Materials
Pencil, dictionary, reference map, crayons or colored pencils, outline map sheet, paper (optional)

Activity
1. Complete the following tasks:
   a. Write the definition of the word *bay*.

   _____

   b. On the outline map, locate and label the Bay of Bengal.
   c. On the outline map, locate and label six (or more) countries.
   d. Write the definition of the word *sea*.

   _____

   e. Locate and label six (or more) seas.
   f. The highest place on earth is a mountain called _____.
   g. Locate and label this mountain on the map.
   h. In the spaces below, draw one animal and one plant that can be found on the continent of Asia.

2. On the back of this sheet or on another sheet of paper, write any other interesting facts that you learned about the continent of Asia. You may also draw illustrations of other interesting animals and plants from the continent.

ASIA

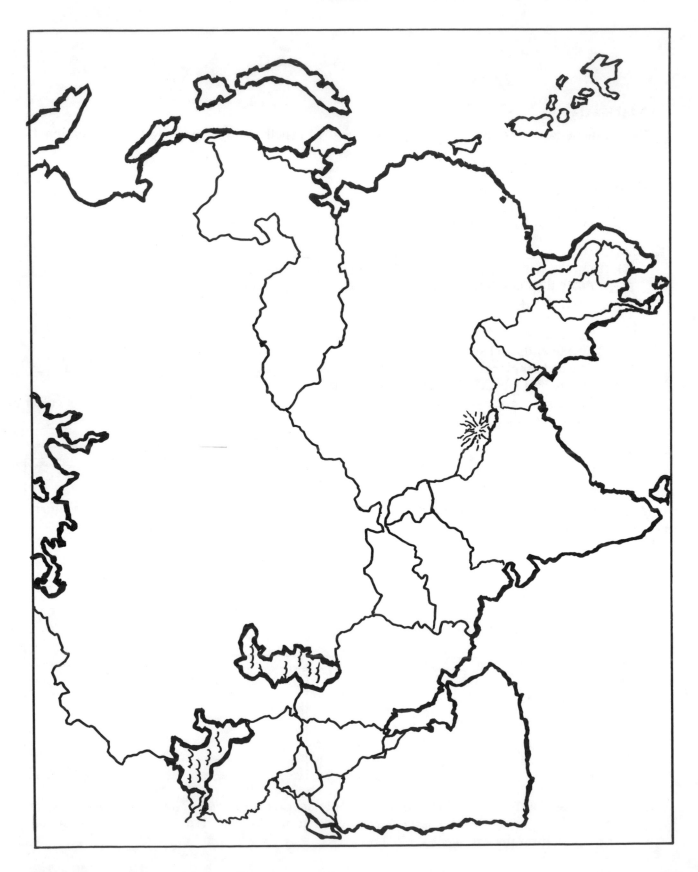

Name _____

AUSTRALIA

Materials
Pencil, dictionary, reference map, crayons or colored pencils, outline map sheet, paper (optional).

Activity
1. Complete the following tasks:
   a. Write the definition of the word *peninsula*.

   _____

   b. On the outline map, label Cape York Peninsula, and Eyre Peninsula..
   c. Write the definition of the word *bight*.

   _____

   d. Label the Great Australian Bight.
   e. Write the definition of the word *cape*.

   _____

   f. Label Cape Leeuwin and Northwest Cape.
   g. Write the definition of the word *reef*.

   _____

   h. Label the Great Barrier Reef.
   i. On the outline map, find and label Canberra, the national capital. Draw a star with a circle around it beside this city.
   j. Label the following states or territories: Western Australia, Northern Territory, Queensland, South Australia, New South Wales, Victoria, and Tasmania.
   k. Label the state and territorial capitals: Sydney, Melbourne, Brisbane, Adelaide, Perth, Darwin, and Hobart.
   l. On the back of this sheet, draw one animal and one plant that can be found on the continent of Australia.

2. On the back of this sheet or on another sheet of paper, write any other interesting facts that you have learned about the continent of Australia. You might want to learn about the government, what the people do for recreation, what products are grown, interesting places to visit, or about the art, literature, or music of the country. You might like to draw illustrations of other plants and animals of the continent.

AUSTRALIA

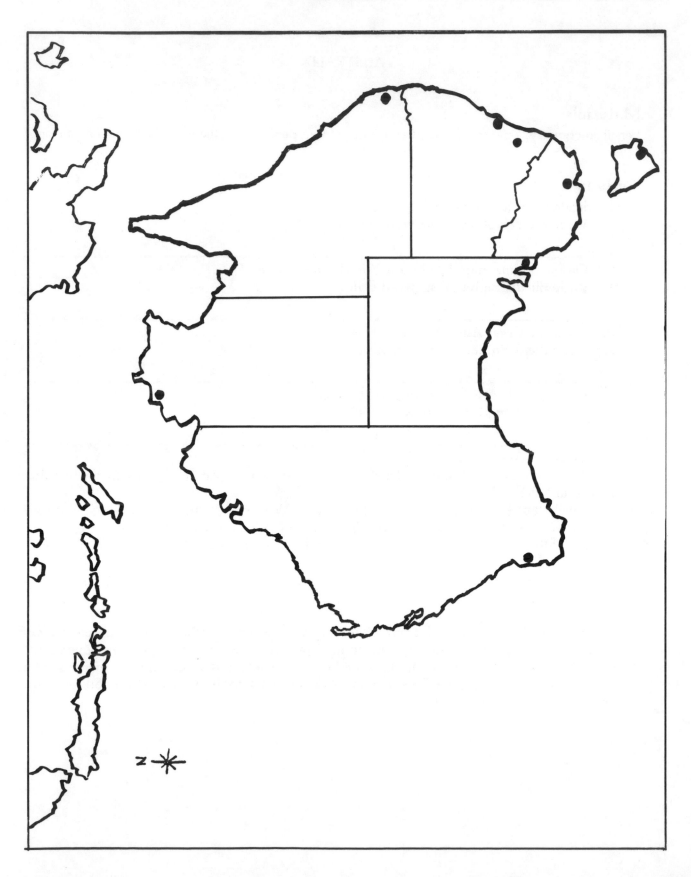

Name _____

EUROPE

Materials

Pencil, dictionary, reference map, outline map sheet, crayons or colored pencils, paper (optional)

Activity

1. Complete the following tasks:
    a. Write the definition of the word *meridian*.

    _____

    b. Draw the prime meridian, or Greenwich meridian, and label it.
    c. Write the definition of the word *longitude*.

    _____

    d. On the outline map, label the following: North Atlantic Ocean, Norwegian Sea, Barents Sea, Baltic Sea, North Sea, Mediterranean Sea.
    e. On the outline map, find the countries below and color them as instructed. Leave all other countries white. Russia (partly in Europe and partly in Asia)—blue; Great Britain (Scotland, England, Northern Ireland, Wales)—blue.

Spain—red	Switzerland—blue
Ireland—green	Poland—brown
Portugal—blue	Denmark—red
France—purple	Italy—green
West Germany—green	Iceland—yellow
Czechoslovakia—pink	Greece—purple
Romania—orange	Norway—pink
East Germany—purple	Sweden—red
Austria—orange	Finland—orange

    f. On the back of this sheet, draw one animal and one plant that can be found on the continent of Europe.

2. Choose one country in Europe to research in greater detail. Learn as many interesting facts as you can. Write the facts that you have learned on the back of this sheet, on another piece of paper, or as your teacher instructs you.

EUROPE

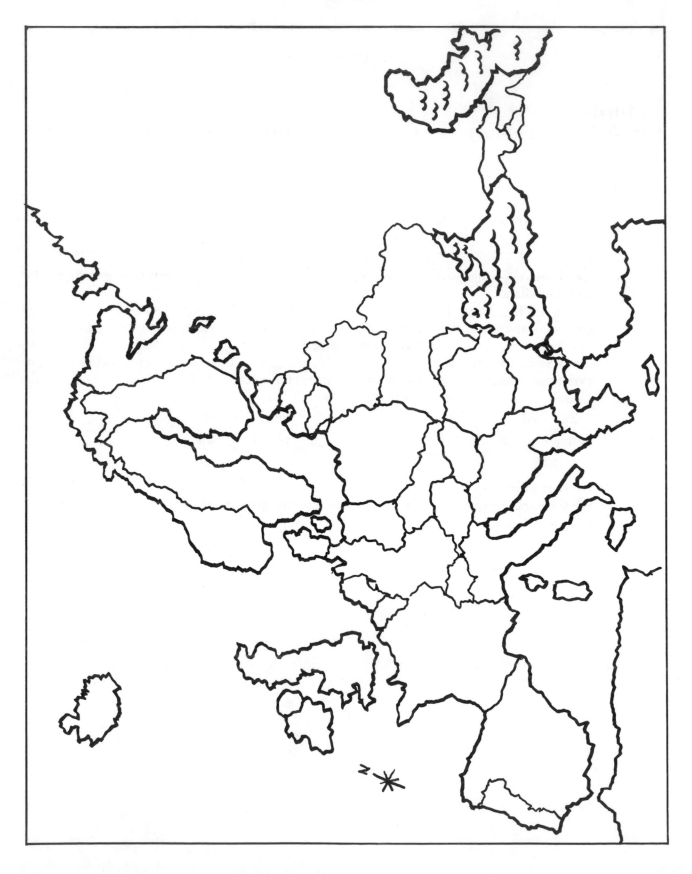

Name _____

NORTH AMERICA

Materials
Dictionary, reference map, pencil, crayons or colored pencils, outline map sheet, paper (optional).

Activity
1. Complete the following tasks:
   a. On the outline map, label the following oceans: Arctic, Pacific, Atlantic.
   b. Greenland, the world's largest island, is part of North America even though it is a province of Denmark. Find and label Greenland on the map.
   c. Label the following islands: Cuba, Baffin Island, Vancouver, the Aleutians, Bermuda, and Newfoundland.
   d. There are five Great Lakes. Lakes Superior, Ontario, Erie, and Huron lie between the countries of Canada and the United States. Find these lakes and label them.
   e. On the outline map, label Lake Winnipeg, and Great Salt Lake. You may extend the names into nearby areas.
   f. Write the definition of the word *gulf*. _____

   _____
   g. Label the Gulf of Mexico.
   h. Write the definition of the word *bay*. _____

   _____
   i. Label Hudson Bay.
   j. On the back of this sheet, draw one animal and one plant that can be found on the continent of North America.

2. On the back of this sheet or on another sheet of paper, write any other interesting facts that you have learned about North America. You may also draw illustrations of other plants and animals of North America.

NORTH AMERICA

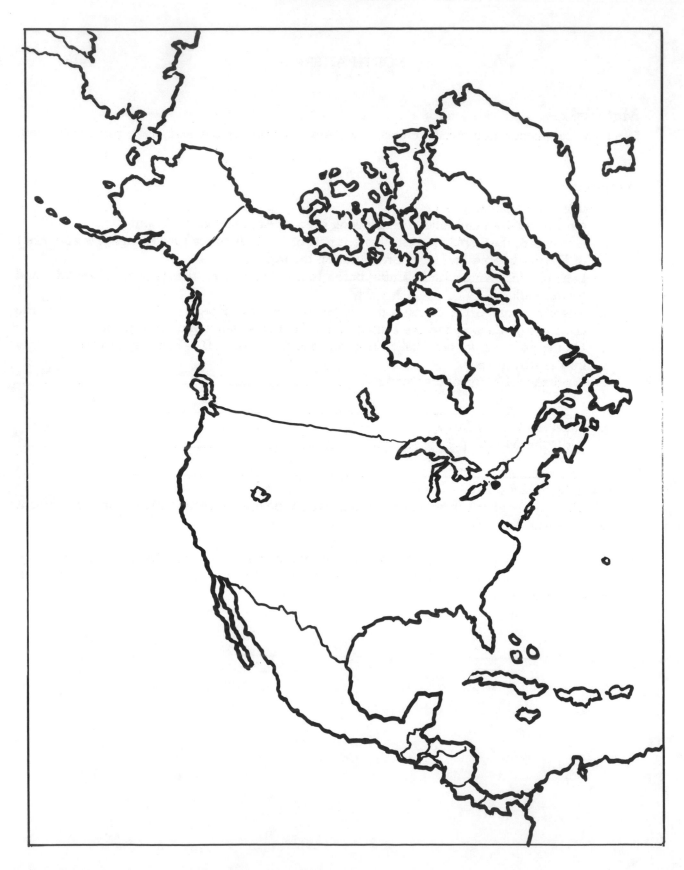

Name _____

SOUTH AMERICA

Materials

Pencil, dictionary, reference map, crayons or colored pencils, outline map sheet, paper (optional).

Activity

1. Complete the following tasks:
    a. On the outline map, label the North Pacific Ocean, the South Pacific Ocean, the North Atlantic Ocean, the South Atlantic Ocean, and the Caribbean Sea.
    b. Write the definition of the word *equator*.

    _____

    c. Draw and label a line to represent the equator.
    d. On the outline map, label the following countries: Argentina, Bolivia, Brazil, Chile, Colombia, Ecuador, French Guiana, Guyana, Paraguay, Peru, Suriname, Uruguay, Venezuela (you may extend the names out into the ocean if necessary).
    e. In the boxes below, draw one animal and one plant that can be found on the continent of South America.

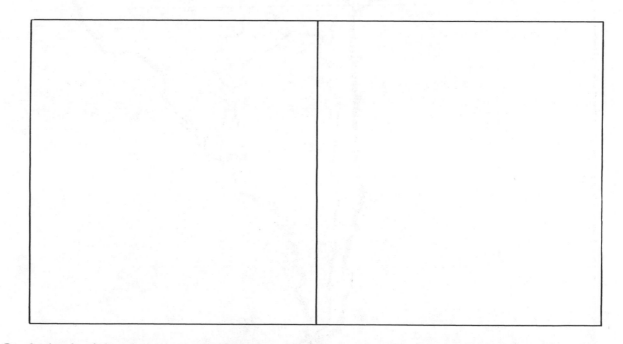

2. On the back of this sheet or on another sheet of paper, write any other interesting facts that you discover about South America. For example, you might discover how people earn their living, the chief products, and what the climate is during the four seasons. You might also draw illustrations of other plants and animals of the continent.

SOUTH AMERICA

BIBLIOGRAPHY

Fradin, Dennis. *Continents (New True Books)*. Chicago: Childrens Press, 1986.

Knowlton, Jack. *Maps and Globes*. Pictures by Harriet Barton. New York: Crowell, 1985.

Ogilvie, Bruce, and Douglas Waitley. *Rand McNally Children's Atlas of the World*. Chicago: Rand McNally, 1985.

AFRICA

Kleeberg, Irene Cumming. *Ethiopia*. New York: Franklin Watts, 1986.

Stark, Al. *Zimbabwe: A Treasure of Africa*. Minneapolis, Minn.: Dillon, 1986.

ANTARCTICA

Sandak, Cass R. *Arctic and Antarctic (New Frontiers)*. New York: Franklin Watts, 1987.

ASIA

McCarthy, Kevin. *Saudi Arabia: A Desert Kingdom*. Minneapolis, Minn.: Dillon, 1986.

Shang, Anthony. *Living in Hong Kong*. Lexington, Mass.: Silver Burdett, 1985.

AUSTRALIA

Gilbreath, Alice. *The Great Barrier Reef: A Treasure in the Sea*. Minneapolis, Minn.: Dillon, 1986.

Gunner, Emily, and Shirley McConky. *A Family in Australia*. New York: Bookwright Press, 1985.

EUROPE

Adler, Ann. *Passport to West Germany*. New York: Franklin Watts, 1986.

Norbrook, Dominique. *Passport to France*. New York: Franklin Watts, 1986.

NORTH AMERICA

Jacobsen, Peter Otto, and Preben Sejer Kristensen. *A Family in Central America*. New York: Bookwright Press, 1985.

May, Robin. *An American Pioneer Family*. Illus. Mark Bergin. Vero Beach, Fla.: Rourke, 1986.

Somonte, Carlos. *We Live in Mexico*. New York: Bookwright Press, 1985.

SOUTH AMERICA

Cross, Wilbur, and Suzanna Cross. *Brazil*. Chicago: Childrens Press, 1984.

Hintz, Martin. *Argentina*. Chicago: Childrens Press, 1985.

Huber, Alex. *We Live in Chile*. New York: Bookwright Press, 1986.

ANSWER KEY

AFRICA

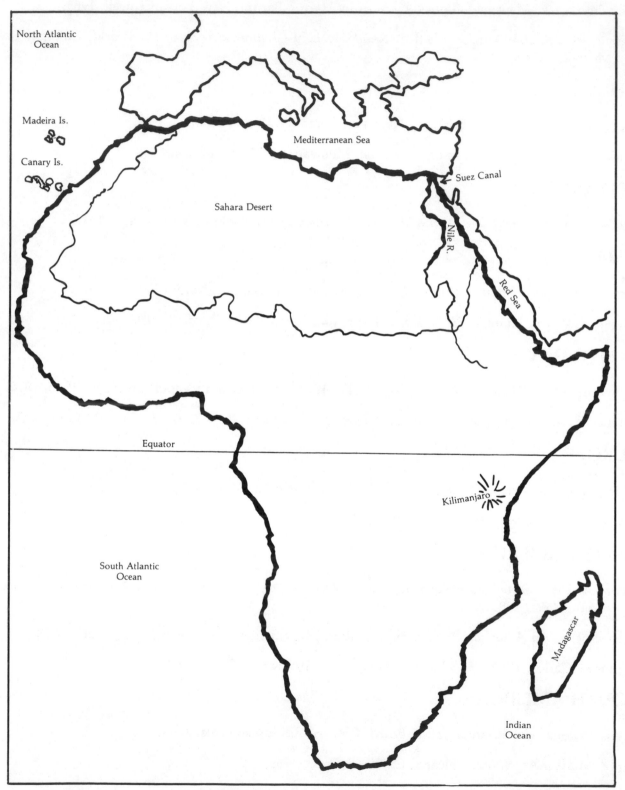

North Atlantic
Ocean

Madeira Is.

Canary Is.

Mediterranean Sea

Suez Canal

Sahara Desert

Nile R.

Red Sea

Equator

Kilimanjaro

South Atlantic
Ocean

Madagascar

Indian
Ocean

ANTARCTICA

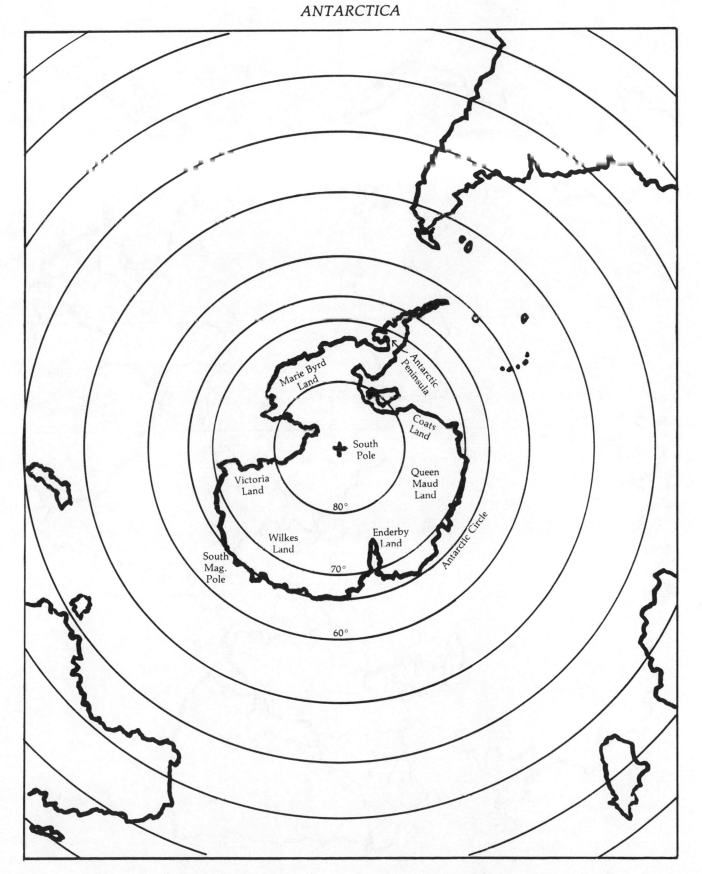

ASIA

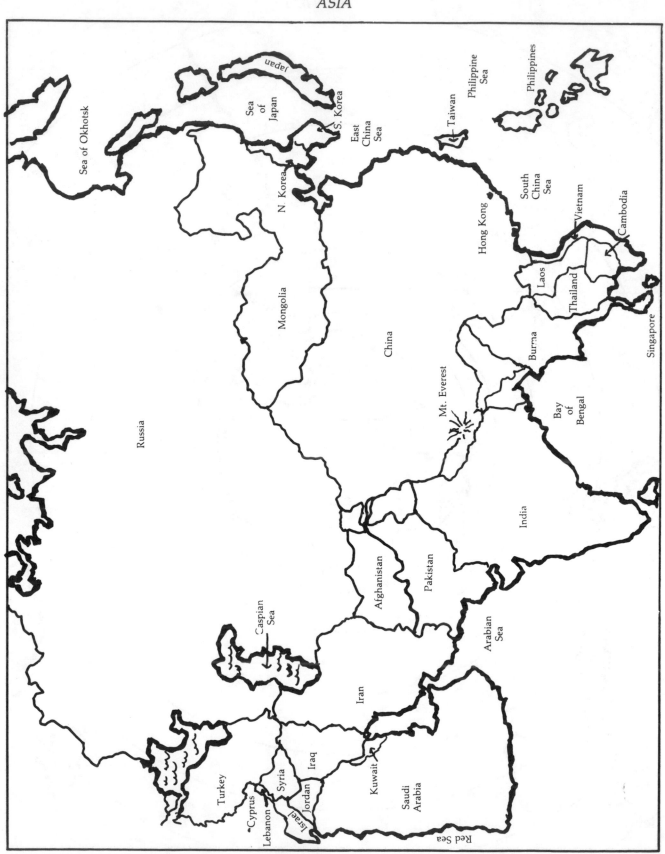

AUSTRALIA

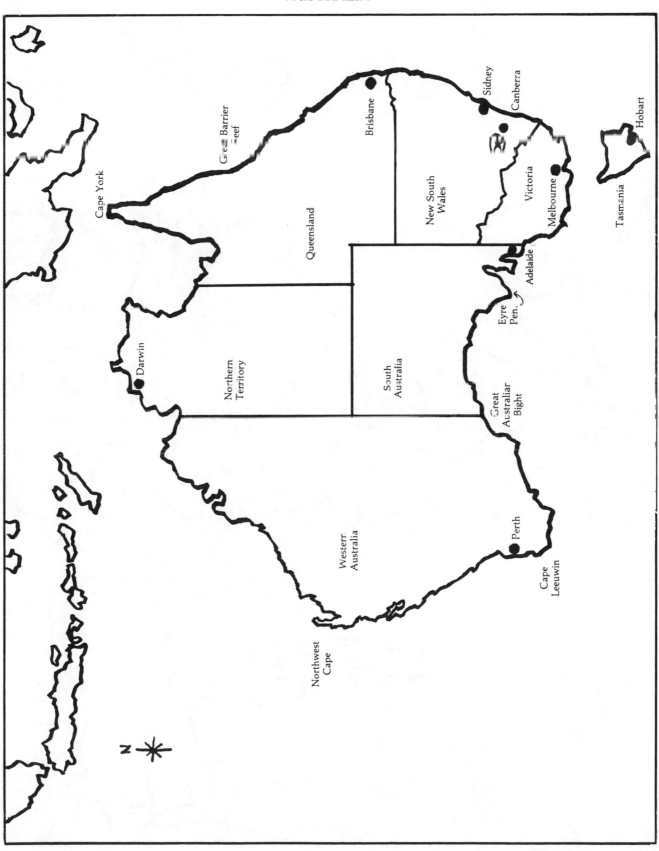

EUROPE

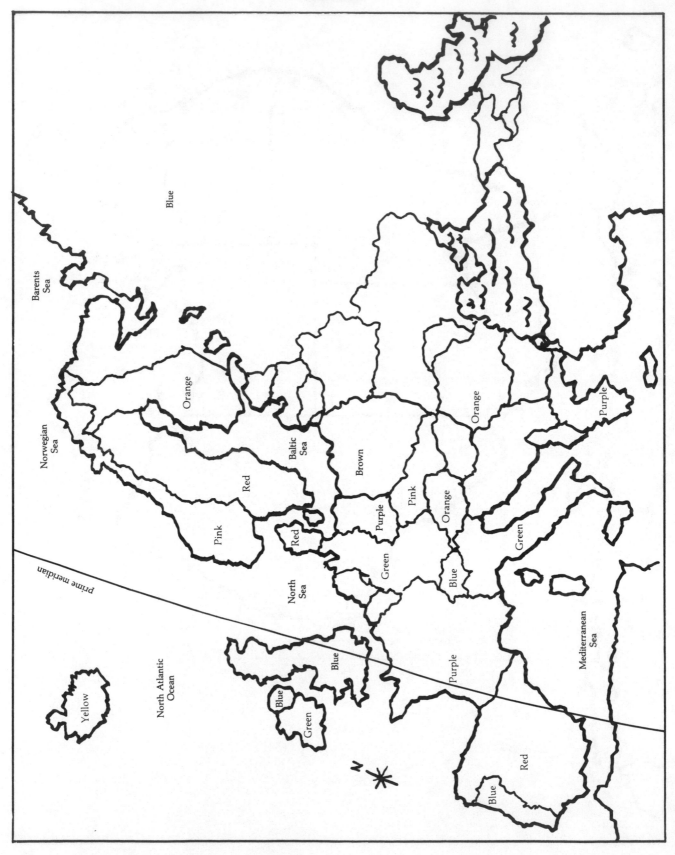

NORTH AMERICA

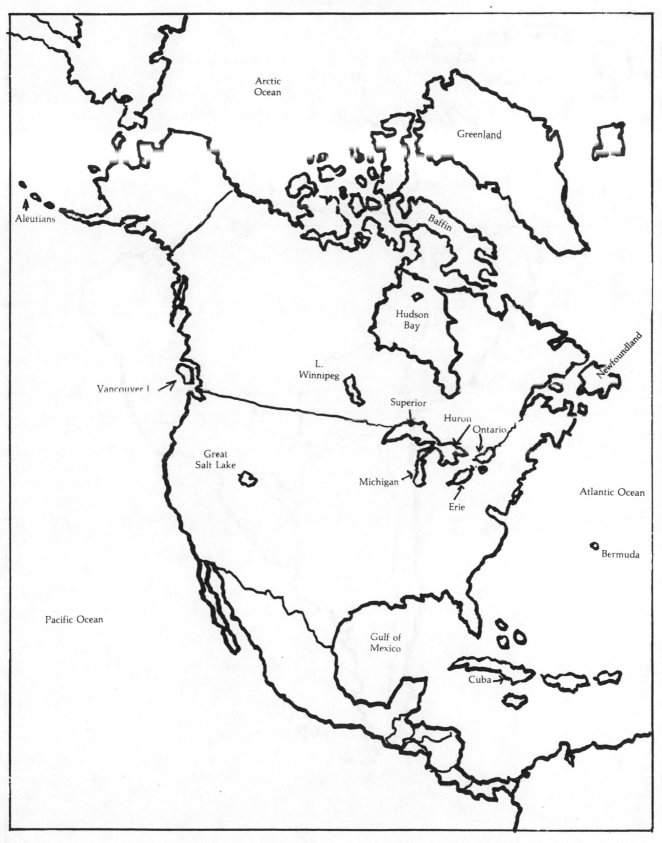

Arctic
Ocean

Greenland

Aleutians

Baffin

Hudson
Bay

L.
Winnipeg

Newfoundland

Vancouver I

Superior

Huron

Ontario

Great
Salt Lake

Michigan

Atlantic Ocean

Erie

Bermuda

Pacific Ocean

Gulf of
Mexico

Cuba

SOUTH AMERICA

North Atlantic Ocean

Caribbean Sea

Venezuela

Guyana

Suriname

French Guiana

Colombia

North Pacific
Ocean

Equator

Ecuador

Brazil

Peru

Bolivia

Paraguay

Chile

Uruguay

South Pacific Ocean

Argentina

South Atlantic Ocean

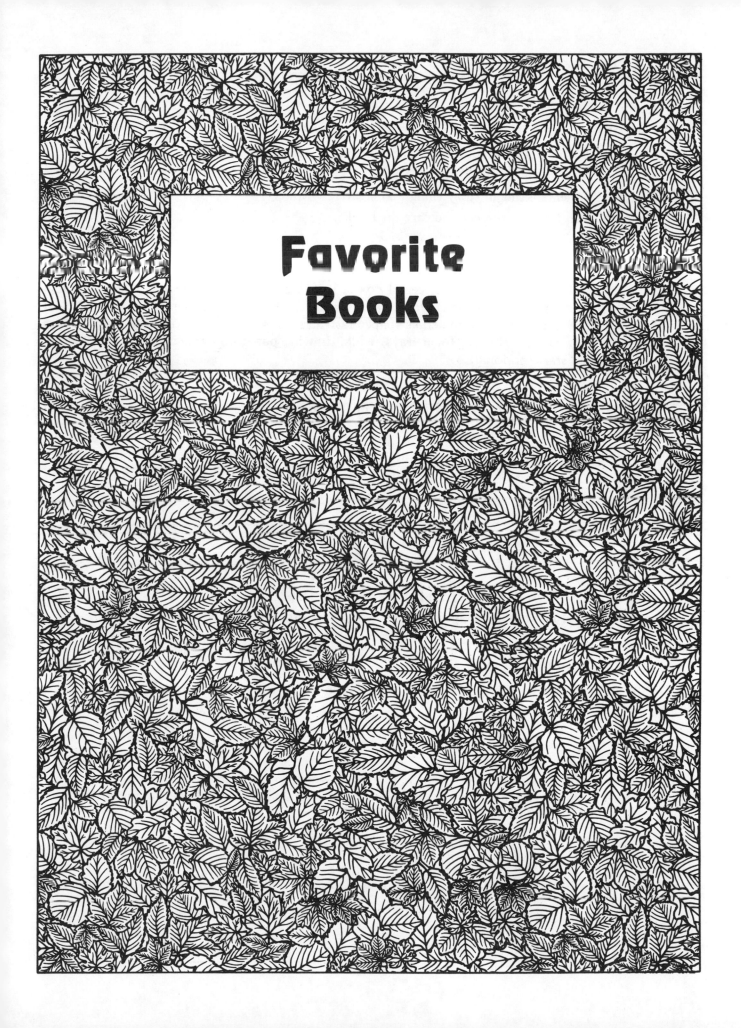

Favorite Books

NOTES TO THE TEACHER

OBJECTIVES

To familiarize students with good literature including Caldecott and Newbery winners.

To foster children's enjoyment of good literature.

To increase students' skills in storytelling and creative writing.

To help children learn to respect and care for books.

MATERIALS

Wallpaper or other decorative paper, cereal boxes, long pipe cleaners, notebook reinforcements, glue, scissors, pencils, markers and crayons, paper punches, construction paper, white paper, ruled paper (optional), book binding materials (paper fasteners, staplers, yarn, notebook rings), long sheets of paper, ruler, tagboard, foam trays, white drawing paper, erasers, mending tape, scrap paper, gummed stars (optional).

TOPIC OF THE WEEK

This introductory activity is to be used with the class as a whole as an introduction to the unit. To allow the students time to read and gather information, it should be used a day or more before they go to Day's End Areas.

DAY'S END AREAS

Paper Crafts—Media Report Holder

The children will make book-shaped pockets in which to store completed media report forms.

Media Report Form

On these forms, the children will record information about the media materials that they have studied.

Paper Crafts—Book Tote-Box

The children will make sturdy boxes with handles in which to carry and store their books.
(For young children you may want to cut the paper or wallpaper to fit the boxes or mark the paper so they are able to cut and fit it themselves.)

Writing—How to Write a Story

The children will learn how to plan good stories. They will then write stories and edit them.

Art—Let's Make a Book

The children will assemble books and decorate the covers, if they wish. They will copy and illustrate the stories they wrote and edited (How to Write a Story) to create self-authored books.

Language Arts—Storytelling

The children will illustrate favorite stories and will use their illustrations as visual aids as they tell their stories to others.

Language Arts—My Favorite Author

The children will gather information about specific authors, discover what books the authors have written, and read some or all of those books.

(You may want to provide gummed stars for the children to use in this activity.)

Art—Literary Awards

The children will design literary awards which they will "award" to books that they consider to be the best and the best illustrated of those that are available to them.

(Show the children a few books bearing the Newbery and Caldecott insignias.)

Book Care—Volunteer Service

The children will explore reasons for and ways of caring for books. They will then perform some book care services.

CULMINATING ACTIVITY

Let each child choose a scene from a favorite book, prepare it, and dramatize it for the class. If more than one character is needed, the children can work together or a single child may assume more than one role.

Name _____

TOPIC OF THE WEEK

Use the dictionary and write the definition of the word *book*.

_____

_____

_____

_____

What words do you associate with the word *book*?

_____   _____

_____   _____

_____   _____

_____   _____

_____   _____

Choose from the books you have read and make a list of your favorites.

_____

_____

_____

_____

_____

_____

_____

_____

_____

_____

Name _____

DAY'S END AREAS

PAPER CRAFTS

Materials
Scissors, glue, crayons and/or markers, scrap paper.

Activity

1. Cut out the book below. Decorate the front as you wish.

2. Using the book as a pattern, cut out a back from a piece of scrap paper.

3. Glue the book and back together along both side edges and the bottom.

4. Complete and cut out a book form from the media report forms page and place it in the holder that you have made.

5. When you have read at least three books, you may draw and color a worm, cut it out, and glue it to the front of your book holder.

MEDIA REPORT FORM

For each item you read or hear, cut out and complete a report card. When you have finished your media report holder, place the completed cards in the holder. Use the back of the card for assignments.

My name is _____

Title of Book or Media Materials

Name of Author

Name of Illustrator

What did you discover in the material that was new to you?

My name is _____

Title of Book or Media Materials

Name of Author

Name of Illustrator

Comments:

My name is _____

Title of Book or Media Materials

Name of Author

Name of Illustrator

Write a paragraph or draw a picture of the most interesting part of what you studied.

My name is _____

Title of Book or Media Materials

Name of Author

Name of Illustrator

Briefly tell about what you studied.

Name _____

BOOK TOTE-BOX

One way to care for your books is to have a box or container in which to carry and store them.

Materials

Wallpaper or other suitable paper, cereal box, long pipe cleaners, notebook reinforcements, glue, scissors, markers, paper punch.

Activity

1. Cover the cereal box with wallpaper or other pretty paper. Glue the paper in place.

2. Write your name on the box with a marker.

3. Punch two holes about 4" apart in the middle of each side of the box (see illustration). Place a notebook reinforcement around each hole.

4. Bend a pipe cleaner through the holes on each side to form two handles. Twist the ends of the pipe cleaners so the handles will be strong (see illustration).

5. Use your tote-box to store and carry your books. Your books will stay clean and neat.

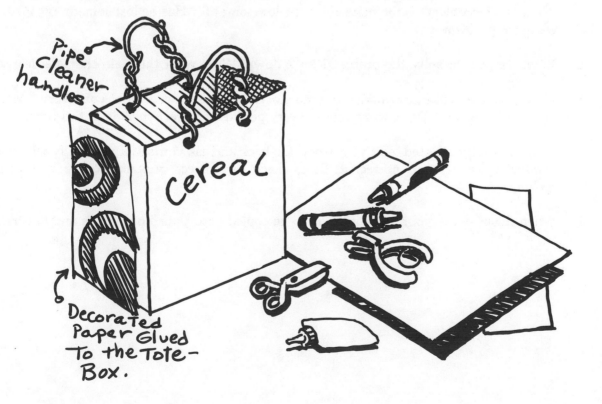

Name _____

CREATIVE WRITING

Good writing is not an accident. It requires a lot of thought and planning.

Materials

Pencil, paper.

Activity

1. Think of three topics about which you might like to write a story. Then choose your favorite topic.

2. Now plan your story. On the back of this sheet, write a title for your story.

3. Every story needs a main character, one around whom the story centers. Choose a main character and write the name of the character.

4. What is the problem? Is the main character lonesome? Ill? Has he lost something? Write down what the problem is.

5. What happens to solve the problem? Jot it down. Write what the main character learned.

6. Now you have a plan, or outline, of your story. Write the first draft of your story. Write what you think and feel. Don't worry about every period or perfect spelling at this time.

7. When you have finished, edit your work. Go back and ask yourself if you really said what you wanted to say. If not, correct it. Then check for correct capitalization, punctuation, and spelling.

8. When this is done, your story is ready to be copied onto your book pages and illustrated.

Name _____

CREATIVE ART

Materials
Construction paper, crayons or markers, white or ruled paper, binding material (paper fasteners, staples, yarn, notebook rings), scissors, long sheets of paper.

Activity

1. Use construction paper (whole sheets or cut to the size you want to make your book) to make book covers. Write the title of your book on the front cover. Write "by" and your name on it, too. Decorate the cover as you wish.

2. Take as many sheets of white or ruled paper as you need to write, illustrate, and bind your book. Cut ½" off one long and one narrow side of the paper to make it a little smaller than the covers.

3. Write your edited story on the pages and illustrate it with pictures. Study books from the library to see the different ways that words and pictures fit on the pages of story books.

4. Assemble your book—front cover, a blank sheet (end paper), a sheet for a title page on which you will write your book title and your name, the story pages, a blank sheet (end paper), and the back cover.

5. Bind your book. You may use paper fasteners, staples, yarn tied through punched holes, or notebook rings (see illustration).

6. You might want to make your book in a shape that relates to your story. Draw a simple outline of the object and cut the covers in that shape. From white or lined paper, cut pages in the same shape. Trim the inside pages a little smaller than the covers.

7. Another kind of book is a fan-folded one. Use a long sheet of paper and fold it in even back and forth folds.

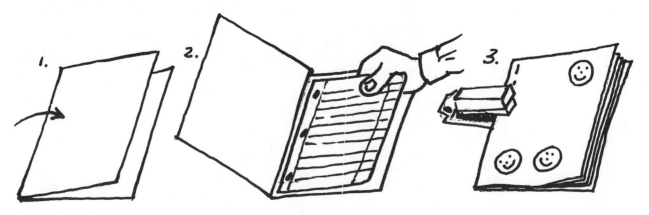

Name _____

LITERARY AWARDS

Many children's books are published each year in the United States. To recognize the best book, an award is given each year. The Newbery Award was first given in 1922. The Caldecott Medal, first given in 1938, recognizes the book with the best illustrations.

Materials

Paper, pencil, crayons or markers, scissors.

Activity

1. On a separate piece of paper, design awards that you would like to place on what you believe are the best book and the most nicely illustrated book in your room.

2. Cut out the awards and clip them to your choices.

3. Why do you think these books should have the awards?

   _____
   _____
   _____
   _____
   _____

4. On the back of this page, make a list of all the Newbery and Caldecott winners you can find.

Name _____

LANGUAGE ARTS

Materials
Scissors, ruler, tagboard, foam tray, white drawing paper, crayons or markers.

Activity

1. Find a story that you would like to share with others.

2. Cut a slit across the center of a foam meat tray.

3. Cut a piece of tagboard as long as the slit plus 1". Cut the piece of tagboard so it is 4½" high.

4. Fold ½" on both short sides of the tagboard. Insert it into the upside down tray to form a card holder.

5. Cut drawing paper into pieces a bit narrower than the folded tagboard and about 5½" high.

6. On one sheet of drawing paper, write the title of the story you have chosen. Decorate the title card, if you wish.

7. Measure with a ruler and mark lightly 3/8" along the top of each story card. Cut 1" tabs (see illustration).

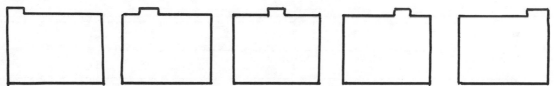

If you have more cards than you have 1" spaces, start again as for the first tab. The tabs make it easy to pick out one story card at a time as you tell your story.

8. Draw pictures on as many sheets as you need to illustrate your story.

9. Insert the finished cards in the correct order into the holder. Then share the story you have prepared with your group or class.

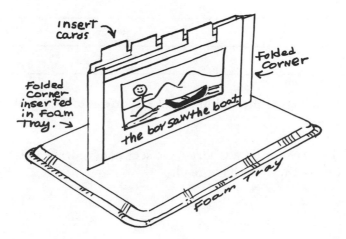

Name _____

MY FAVORITE AUTHOR

Materials
Pencil, crayons or markers, white paper (optional).

Activity

1. Choose an author whose books you enjoy. Using encyclopedias or other media sources, learn about the author. Write a summary of the information you have gathered.

   _____

   _____

   _____

   _____

   _____

   _____

   _____

   _____

   _____

2. Make a list of this author's books. Look in your library. Use the card catalog to help you.

   _____

   _____

   _____

   _____

   _____

   _____

3. Read as many as you can of the author's books. Draw a star (or apply a gummed star) beside the titles you have read.

4. On the back of this sheet or on a separate piece of paper, draw a picture (or pictures) about one or more of the books that you have read.

Name _____

VOLUNTEER ACTIVITY

Materials
Erasers, mending tape.

In your group, discuss the importance of taking care of books. List your reasons.

_____   _____

_____   _____

_____   _____

Discuss and make a list of things you can do to care for books.

_____   _____

_____   _____

_____   _____

Look up the word *volunteer* in the dictionary. What does it mean?

_____

_____

VOLUNTEER SERVICE. Now find in the library or your room some books that are in need of care. Do what is needed to care for them. Make a list of the things that you did.

_____   _____

_____   _____

_____   _____

_____   _____

How did you feel while you were serving as a book care volunteer?

_____

_____

_____

On the back of this sheet, list other volunteer services that you have heard about.
(You might want to interview someone who performs a volunteer service and share this with your class at the end of the unit.)

BIBLIOGRAPHY—NEWBERY MEDAL WINNERS

Year	Author	Title
1922	Hendrik Van Loon	The Story of Mankind
1923	Hugh Lofting	The Voyages of Doctor Dolittle
1924	Charles Hawes	The Dark Frigate
1925	Charles Finger	Tales from Silver Lands
1926	Arthur Chrisman	Shen of the Sea
1927	Will James	Smoky
1928	Dham Mukerji	Gay-Neck
1929	Eric P. Kelly	The Trumpeter of Krakow
1930	Rachel Field	Hitty, Her First Hundred Years
1931	Elizabeth Coatsworth	The Cat Who Went to Heaven
1932	Laura Armer	Waterless Mountain
1933	Elizabeth Lewis	Young Fu of the Upper Yangtze
1934	Cornelia Meigs	Invincible Louisa
1935	Monica Shannon	Dobry
1936	Carol Brink	Caddie Woodlawn
1937	Ruth Sawyer	Roller Skates
1938	Kate Seredy	White Stag
1939	Elizabeth Enright	Thimble Summer
1940	James Daugherty	Daniel Boone
1941	Armstrong Sperry	Call It Courage
1942	Walter Edmonds	The Matchlock Gun
1943	Elizabeth Gray	Adam of the Road
1944	Esther Forbes	Johnny Tremain
1945	Robert Lawson	Rabbit Hill
1946	Lois Lenski	Strawberry Girl
1947	Carolyn Bailey	Miss Hickory
1948	William Pène du Bois	Twenty-One Balloons
1949	Marguerite Henry	King of the Wind
1950	Marguerite de Angeli	Door in the Wall
1951	Elizabeth Yates	Amos Fortune, Free Man
1952	Eleanor Estes	Ginger Pye
1953	Ann Nolan Clark	Secret of the Andes
1954	Joseph Krumgold	...And Now Miguel
1955	Meindert DeJong	The Wheel on the School
1956	Jean Lee Latham	Carry On, Mr. Bowditch
1957	Virginia Sorenson	Miracles on Maple Hill
1958	Harold Keith	Rifles for Waite
1959	Elizabeth Speare	The Witch of Blackbird Pond
1960	Joseph Krumgold	Onion John
1961	Scott O'Dell	Island of the Blue Dolphins
1962	Elizabeth Speare	The Bronze Bow
1963	Madeleine L'Engle	A Wrinkle in Time
1964	Emily Neville	It's Like This, Cat
1965	Maia Wojciechowska	Shadow of the Bull
1966	Elizabeth de Trevino	I, Juan de Pareja
1967	Irene Hunt	Up a Road Slowly
1968	Elaine Konigsburg	From the Mixed-Up Files of Mrs. Basil E. Frankweiler
1969	Lloyd Alexander	High King
1970	William Armstrong	Sounder
1971	Betsy Byars	Summer of the Swans
1972	R. C. O'Brien	Mrs. Frisby and the Rats of Nimh
1973	Jean George	Julie of the Wolves
1974	Paula Fox	The Slave Dancer
1975	Virginia Hamilton	M. C. Higgins, The Great
1976	Susan Cooper	The Grey King
1977	Mildred Taylor	Roll of Thunder, Hear My Cry
1978	Katherine Paterson	Bridge to Terabithia
1979	Ellen Raskin	The Westing Game
1980	Joan Blos	Gathering of Days
1981	Katherine Paterson	Jacob Have I Loved
1982	Nancy Willard	Visit to William Blake's Inn
1983	Cynthia Voigt	Dicey's Song
1984	Beverly Cleary	Dear Mr. Henshaw
1985	Robin McKinley	The Hero and the Crown
1986	Patricia MacLachlin	Sarah, Plain and Tall
1987	Sid Fleischman	The Whipping Boy
1988	Russell Freedman	A Pluto (Biography)

Note: The Newbery Medal goes to the most distinguished contribution to American literature for children published during the preceding year.

Flowers

NOTES TO THE TEACHER

OBJECTIVES

To familiarize students with a number of common flowers.

To increase students' appreciation of the beauty of flowers in their lives and as gifts to others.

To help students understand the anatomy and growth of flowers.

MATERIALS

Scissors, glue, crayons and markers, pipe cleaners, styrofoam cups, paper punches, construction paper, pencils, ½ pint milk containers (optional), decorative paper for covering milk cartons (optional), dwarf marigold seeds, potting soil or light garden soil, tissue paper in several flowery colors, green tissue paper, small margarine tubs and lids, twigs, staplers, green clay, red or yellow clay.

TOPIC OF THE WEEK

This introductory activity is to be used with the class as a whole as an introduction to the unit. To allow the students time to read and gather information, it should be used a day or more before they go to Day's End Areas.

DAY'S END AREAS

Paper Crafts—Media Report Holder

The children will cut out, decorate, and assemble seed packets in which to store media report forms.

Media—Media Report Forms

On these forms the children will record information about the media materials that they have studied. They will store the completed forms in their seed packet holders.

Research—Flowers to Color

The children will research to learn how to color a number of flowers and will then color the flowers correctly. Reproduce blank cards in bird unit section for children to use for their own flowers.

Science—Flower Parts

The children will draw illustrations and label the parts of a flower.

Science—Grow a Flower

The children will plant marigold seeds and keep records of the growth of the plants.

Career—Floral Shop

The children will make bouquets of tissue paper flowers.
(The children can probably bring their own small margarine tubs and twigs for this project.)

Poetry—A Flower Bouquet

The children will learn about Haiku as a poetic form. They will make flower-decorated door hangers and will write original Haiku poems on them.
(You might want to share some examples of Haiku with the children before they do this activity.)

CULMINATING ACTIVITY

If possible, the class might visit a floral shop, or someone from a floral shop might be invited to come in and speak to the students.

The children might make creative gift cards to be used when they give the hangers, the flowers they have grown, or their floral shop creations to friends or family members.

Name _____

TOPIC OF THE WEEK

Use the dictionary to learn the meaning of the word *flower*. Write the meaning. _____
_____
_____
_____

What words do you associate with the word *flower*?

_____   _____
_____   _____
_____   _____
_____   _____
_____   _____

Make a list of any articles or stories about the topic that are available to you from any media source (books, magazines, filmstrips, computer disks, tapes).

_____
_____
_____
_____
_____
_____
_____
_____
_____
_____
_____

Name _____

DAY'S END AREAS

PAPER CRAFTS

Materials
Scissors, glue, crayons or markers.

Activity
1. Cut out the seed packet.

2. Using crayons or markers, decorate the front of your packet.

3. Fold the packet together on the lines. Glue along the edges as shown.

4. Fold on the dotted line to form the flap.

5. When you have completed media report forms, store them in your seed packet.

Fold #1

Fold #4

Fold #3

Fold #2

Fold #1, Spread glue on other side of #1.

Fold #2, onto Flap #1 and wet glue.

Spread glue on #3 and Fold onto Flap #2.

Fold #4, but do not Glue it.

3.

2.

1.

MEDIA REPORT FORM

For each item you read or hear, cut out and complete a report card. When you have finished your media report holder, place the completed cards in the holder. Use the back of the card for assignments.

My name is _____

Title of Book or Media Materials

Name of Author

Name of Illustrator

What did you discover in the material that was new to you?

My name is _____

Title of Book or Media Materials

Name of Author

Name of Illustrator

Comments:

My name is _____

Title of Book or Media Materials

Name of Author

Name of Illustrator

Write a paragraph or draw a picture of the most interesting part of what you studied.

My name is _____

Title of Book or Media Materials

Name of Author

Name of Illustrator

Briefly tell about what you studied.

Name _____

RESEARCH

Materials
Crayons or markers, two sheets of flower cards, blank card sheet (optional).

Activity
1. Use encyclopedias, flower books, magazines or other media sources to learn the proper colors of these flowers.

2. Then color each flower correctly.

3. If you want to draw and color some other flowers that you choose, use a blank card sheet.

Sunflower

Poinsettia

Fuchsia

Daffodil

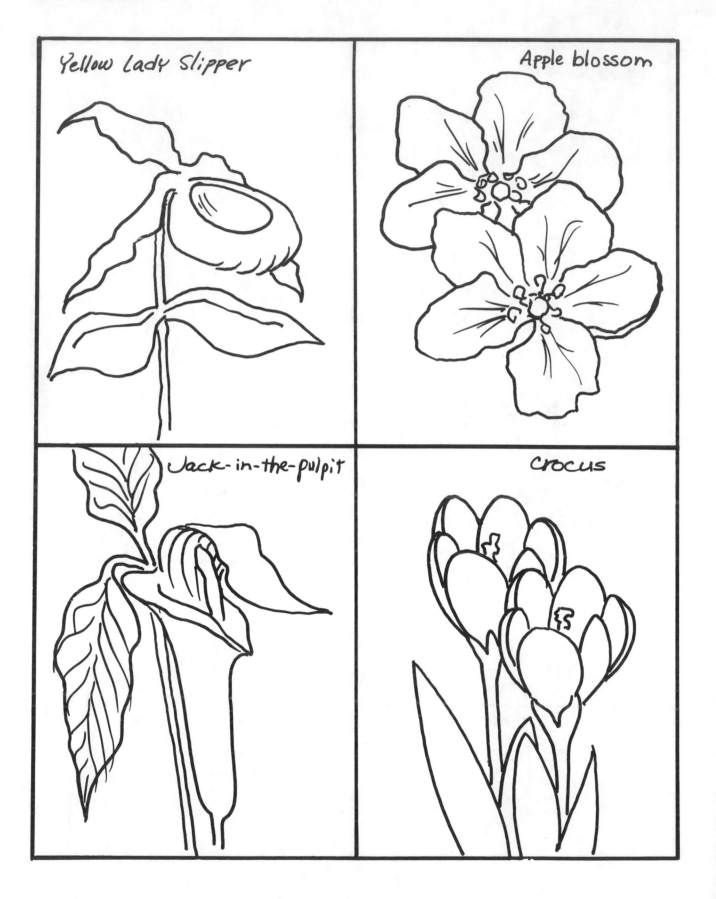

Yellow Lady Slipper

Apple blossom

Jack-in-the-pulpit

Crocus

Name _____

SCIENCE

Materials
Pencil.

Activity

1. In the space below the line, draw this flower larger than the illustration.

2. Label the parts of the flower.

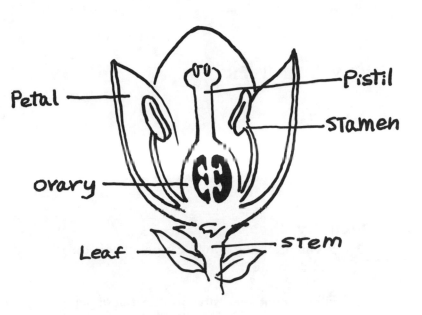

Petal — Pistil — Stamen — Ovary — Leaf — Stem

Name _____

GROW A FLOWER

Materials
Styrofoam cups or ½ pint milk containers, paper for decorating the cartons (optional), scissors, dwarf marigold seeds, potting soil or light garden dirt, pencil, crayons or markers.

Activity
1. If you are using a milk carton, cut off the top section. You may cover your carton with paper and decorate it.

2. Fill the container three-fourths full of soil.

3. Place a marigold seed in the center and cover it with ¼" of soil.

4. Keep the soil moist, but not too wet. Place it in a sunny window.

GROWTH RECORD

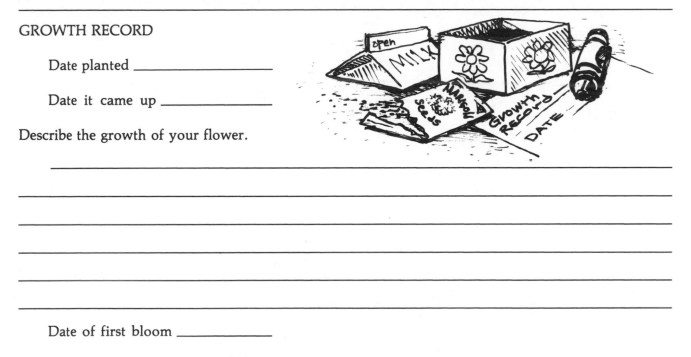

Date planted _____

Date it came up _____

Describe the growth of your flower.

_____

_____

_____

_____

_____

_____

Date of first bloom _____

On the back of this sheet, draw and color a picture of the bloom.

Name _____

CAREERS

Materials
Several colors of tissue paper for flowers, green tissue paper, small margarine tub and lid, small twigs, paper punch, stapler, green clay, red or yellow clay, scissors, glue.

Activity

1. Fold the lid of the margarine tub in half and, with a paper punch, make several holes. Place the lid on the tub.

2. Layer 13-15 pieces of colored tissue (2" x 2") and staple them in the center. Use a paper punch to punch a hole in the center of the layered tissue.

3. Cut circle-shaped petals making the edges irregular and flower-like. Pinch each petal in the center to shape it. Separate the petals gently.

4. Roll a small ball of green clay (¼") and push it onto a twig. Place the tissue flower on the twig and push it against the ball of clay. Roll another small ball of clay (red or yellow) for the flower center and push it onto the end of the twig and against the flower. Make as many flowers as you wish.

5. Fan-fold a piece of another color of tissue and cut a small rounded shape (½" to ¾"). Be sure to leave the tissue attached at the folds (see illustration). Punch a hole in the center and slip it onto a twig. It will fan out the length of the twig to make a flower. Make as many as you wish to have in your bouquet.

6. Push each twig through a hole that you punched in the lid of the margarine tub.

7. Cut leaves freehand from green tissue paper. Place a dot of glue on one end of each leaf and stick the leaves to the twigs in an attractive arrangement.

8. Think of and list ways that you can use your bouquet. Use the back of this sheet.

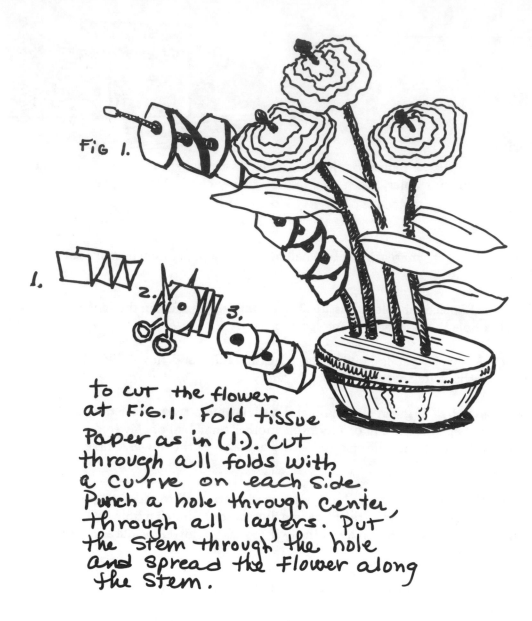

FIG 1.

1.

2.

3.

to cut the flower
at Fig.1. Fold tissue
paper as in (1.). Cut
through all folds with
a curve on each side.
Punch a hole through center,
through all layers. Put
the stem through the hole
and spread the flower along
the stem.

Name _____

POETRY (HAIKU)

A flower bouquet
Is a sign of love and care
That good friends may share.

Writers often express their most intense feelings through poetry. Poetry is often written about things in nature, including the beauty of flowers. Haiku is a form of poetry that came from Japan and follows a set form: five syllables in line one, seven in line two, and five in line three.

Materials

Scissors, pencil, crayons or markers, paper.

Activity

1. Cut out the doorknob hanger pattern.

2. On another sheet of paper, write a poem in Haiku and copy it onto the hanger.

3. Decorate the other side of the hanger with a bouquet of flowers. Use your hanger as a gift.

4. If you wish and have time, make more hangers from whatever materials you desire.

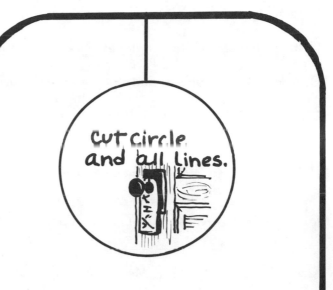

BIBLIOGRAPHY

Burnett, Frances Hodgson. *The Secret Garden*. New York: Harper and Row, 1985.

Cooney, Barbara. *Miss Rumphius*. New York: Viking Press, 1982.

Dowden, Anne Ophelia. *State Flowers*. New York: Thomas Y. Crowell, 1978.

Gunthorp, Dale. *The Life of Plants*. Illus. Stephen Bennet et al. Adapted from the original text by John Simmons. Jean Cooper, Consultant. Lexington, Mass.: Silver Burdett Co., 1978.

Hogan, Paula Z. *The Life Cycle of the Dandelion*. Illus. Yoshi Miyake. Milwaukee, Wis.: Raintree Children's Books, 1979.

Johnson, Sylvia A. *Morning Glories*. Photos by Yuko Sato. Minneapolis, Minn.: Lerner Publications, 1985.

Kazue, Mizumura. *Flower, Moon, Snow: A Book of Haiku*. New York: Harper and Row (Crowell), 1977.

Kirkpatrick, Rena K. *Flowers*. Illus. Annabel Milne and Peter Stebbing. Milwaukee, Wis.: Raintree Children's Books, 1985.

Krasilovsky, Phyllis. *The First Tulips in Holland*. Illus. S. D. Schindler. Garden City, N.Y.: Doubleday & Co., 1982.

Lauber, Patricia. *From Flower to Flower*. Photos by Jerome Wexler. New York: Crown Publishers, Inc., 1986.

———. *Seeds*. Photos by Jerome Wexler. New York: Crown Publishers, Inc., 1981.

Lerner, Carol. *Flowers of a Woodland Spring*. New York: William Morrow and Co., 1979.

Leutscher, Alfred. *Flowering Plants (Action Science)*. New York: Franklin Watts, 1984.

McMillan, Bruce. *Counting Wildflowers*. New York: Lothrop, Lee & Shepard, 1986.

Pringle, Laurence. *Being a Plant*. Illus. Robin Brickman. New York: Thomas Y. Crowell, 1983.

Svatos, Ladislav. *Dandelion*. Garden City, N.Y.: Doubleday & Co., Inc., 1976.

Welch, Martha McKeen. *Sunflower!* New York: Dodd, Mead & Co., 1980.

Zim, Herbert Spencer. *Flowers: A Guide to Familiar American Wildflowers*. New York: Goldcraft Western, 1961.

Humor

NOTES TO THE TEACHER

OBJECTIVES

To help students understand the value of positive attitudes to health and the enjoyment of life.

To help students learn to appreciate humor in life and literature.

MATERIALS

Crayons and markers, scissors, glue, yarn (optional), paper punches, pencils, smiley face stickers (optional), construction paper, half sheets of lined theme paper, staplers, large pieces of brown or yellow paper (kraft, construction, or from a roll), rulers, comic strips, heavy paper or tagboard, and envelopes.

TOPIC OF THE WEEK

This introductory activity is to be used as an introduction to the unit. To allow the students time to read and gather background information, it should be used a day or more before the children go to Day's End Areas. During discussion, stress the health benefits of positive attitudes.

DAY'S END AREAS

Paper Crafts—Media Report Record

The children will cut out and assemble mouse and cheese decorations on which to keep track of the media materials they have studied.

(Duplicate the mouse pattern on gray or light brown paper and the cheese pattern on yellow paper. You might want to provide smiley face stickers or simply have the students draw smiley faces on the "Topic of the Week" sheet beside the titles of the materials they have studied.)

Art—Joke or Riddle Book

The children will make and illustrate books of favorite jokes or riddles.

Art—Be an Illustrator

The children will copy and illustrate favorite poems.

Writing—My Tall Tale

The children will cut large pancakes from brown or yellow paper and write original tall tales on the pancakes.

(Try to read a Paul Bunyan story to the children before they begin this activity. They would enjoy writing with jumbo pencils, if possible. A large Paul Bunyan sitting at a table eating the "pancakes" [tall tales] would make a nice bulletin board or wall display.)

Phonics and Writing—Silly Sentences

The children will use particular sounds to write alliterative sentences.

(You might want to choose sounds you are studying for the children to use in their sentences and/or let them choose a given number to use.)

Language Arts—Cartoon Sequences

The children will cut cartoon strips apart, mix up the pieces, and try to put the stories back into the correct sequence.

CULMINATING ACTIVITY

Let the children share their silly sentences and tall tales or a few favorite jokes from the books they prepared. After the sharing time, you might serve Giggle cookies (Nabisco, twenty-four per box) or provide plain sugar cookies and a few tubes of decorating gel or icing (Betty Crocker) and let the children take turns creating their own smiley-faced cookies.

Name _____

TOPIC OF THE WEEK
_____

Use a dictionary to find the meaning of the word *humor*. Write it below. _____
_____
_____

What words do you associate with the word *humor*?

_____   _____
_____   _____
_____   _____
_____   _____
_____   _____

Make a list of humorous articles or stories that are available to you from any media source (books, magazines, filmstrips, computer disks, tapes).

_____
_____
_____
_____
_____
_____
_____
_____

Find the meaning of the word *attitude*. Write it below.

_____
_____
_____

People with *positive* attitudes are those who see the good sides of other people and situations. They expect things to go right or get better. They tend to smile a lot. They don't complain about everything. A *negative* attitude is the opposite of a positive one. On the back of this page, write a paragraph telling the advantages of having a positive attitude.

Name _____

DAY'S END AREAS

PAPER CRAFTS

Materials
Mouse pattern, cheese pattern, crayons or markers, scissors, glue, yarn (optional), paper punch, pencil, smiley face stickers (if provided).

Activity
1. Cut out the cheese design.

2. Color the mouse's tongue and cut out the mouse. Cut around the mouse's paws, but leave them attached (see illustration).

3. Glue the mouse onto the cheese so that the paws are in front and the tail wraps around the edge and over the front side edge of the cheese. If you wish, you may cut off the paper tail and glue on a yarn tail. Wrap and glue the yarn tail as you like.

4. Each time you read a humorous book or article, listen to a tape, or view a filmstrip or disk, punch a hole in the cheese with a paper punch.

5. Each time you punch a hole in the cheese, put a smiley face on the "Topic of the Week" sheet beside the title of the media material you studied.

Glue cheese in front of mouse.

Punch holes in cheese according to directions.

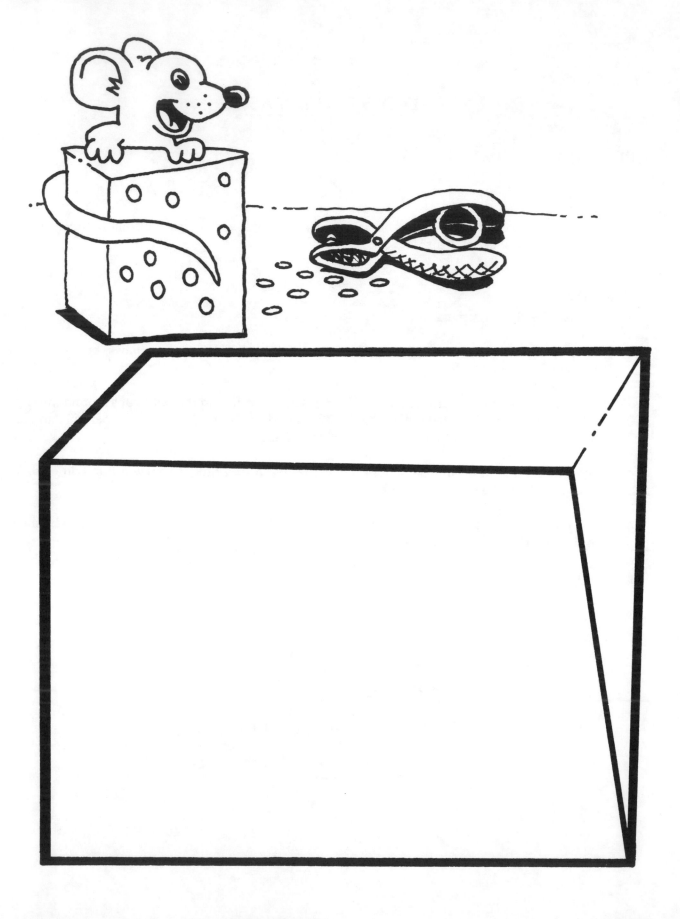

Name _____

CREATIVE ART

Materials
Construction paper, 4-6 pieces of lined paper, stapler, crayons and/or markers, pencil.

Activity

1. Fold a sheet of construction paper in half to form the cover of your book.

2. Lay 4 to 6 sheets of lined paper together evenly. Insert inside the folded construction paper.

3. Staple your book together along the fold (see illustration).

4. Decorate the front of your joke book.

5. Write a joke or riddle—your own or a favorite one from a book—on each page and draw a picture on the page to illustrate it.

Name _____

BE AN ILLUSTRATOR

Materials
Markers or crayons, pencil.

Activity

1. Choose a humorous poem. In your best handwriting, copy it in the space below.

2. On the back of this page, make an original (something you've thought of yourself, not a copied idea) illustration to go with the poem.

_____
_____
_____
_____
_____
_____
_____
_____
_____
_____
_____
_____
_____
_____
_____
_____

Name _____

CREATIVE WRITING

A tall tale is a story that is exaggerated. This means that facts are made greater than they really are. People and animals do impossible things. Things are larger than in real life. This exaggeration creates humor.

Materials

A piece of light brown or yellow paper, ruler, scissors, pencil.

Activity

1. Cut a very large pancake from light brown or yellow paper.

2. Use creases or a ruler to make lines on the pancake.

3. On your pancake, write an original tall tale about Paul Bunyan.

Write your tall tale on the creases formed on the pancake.

Name _____

PHONICS AND WRITING

Bl

Alliteration is the use of the same sound over and over at the beginning of words in a sentence or line of poetry. (Tired Tillie talked too much.)

Pr

Sc

BR

Materials

Pencil.

Th

CH

Activity

1. Circle the letters that represent the sounds you will use in writing silly sentences. Your teacher may tell you which sounds to circle or let you choose a certain number of sounds.

2. Write a silly sentence for each sound you circled.

Sk

Cl

Sl

Cr

Sm

Dr

Sn

Fl

Sp

Fr

St

Gl

Sw

Gr

Th

Kn

Tr

Tw

Ph

Wh

Pl

Wr

my 🐱 crawls along the carpet to creep up on 🐦🐦 .

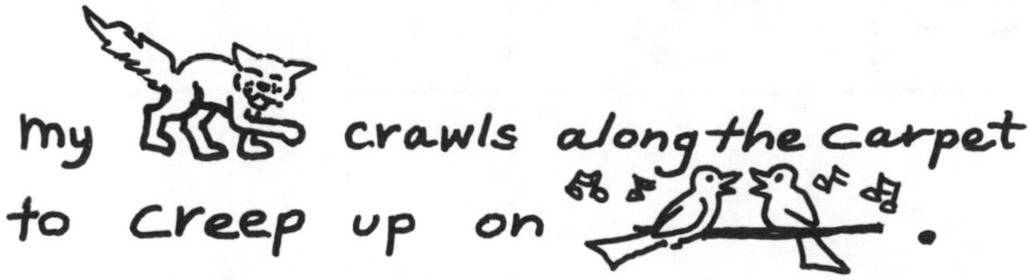

Name _____

LANGUAGE ARTS

Sequence is the order in which things happen or belong. It is often important in understanding a story.

Materials

Comic strip, glue, scissors, heavy paper or tagboard, envelope, pencil.

Activity

1. Find a comic strip that you like.

2. Glue it on a piece of heavy paper or tagboard.

3. When the glue is dry, cut the strip apart on the lines between scenes.

4. Number each piece on the back in the correct order before you cut the strip apart. Write your name on the back of each piece.

5. Mix up the pieces. Try to put the story back into the correct sequence. After you've finished, check your work by looking at the numbers on the backs of the pieces.

6. Exchange with your friends and try to sequence one another's comics.

7. A plain envelope will keep your pieces together so that you can continue to enjoy your comic strip.

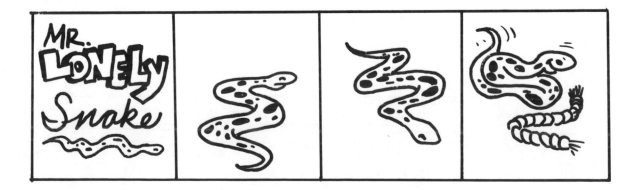

BIBLIOGRAPHY

Alden, Compiler. *Still More Knock-Knocks, Limericks, and Other Silly Sayings*. Chicago: Childrens Press, 1986.

Bishop, Ann. *Hello, Mr. Chips! Computer Jokes and Riddles*. Illus. Jerry Warshaw. Chicago: Albert Whitman and Co., 1982.

Byars, Betsy. *The Computer Nut*. Illus. Guy Byars. Rutherford, N.J.: Viking Kestrel, 1984.

Corbett, Scott. *Down with Wimps!* Illus. Larry Ross. New York: E. P. Dutton, 1984.

Dexter, Catherine. *Gertie's Green Thumb*. Illus. Ellen Eagle. New York: Macmillan Publishing Co., 1983.

Funai, Mamoru. *Cartoons for Kids*. Englewood Cliffs, N.J.: Prentice-Hall, Inc., 1977.

Gackenbach, Dick. *Timid Timothy's Tongue Twisters*. New York: Holiday House, 1986.

Heide, Florence Parry. *Treehorn's Treasure*. Illus. Edward Gorey. New York: Holiday House, 1981.

Howe, James. *The Celery Stalks at Midnight*. Illus. Leslie Morrill. New York: Atheneum, 1983.

Kessler, Leonard. *Old Turtle's Riddle and Joke Book*. New York: Greenwillow Books, 1986.

Lisle, Janet Taylor. *The Dancing Cats of Applesap*. Illus. Joelle Shefts. New York: Bradbury Press, 1984.

Maestro, Giulio. *What's a Frank Frank? Tasty Homograph Riddles*. Boston: Clarion Books, 1984.

Marshall, James. *Taking Care of Carruthers*. New York: Houghton Mifflin, 1981.

Phillips, Louis. *How Do You Get a Horse out of the Bathtub?* Illus. James Stevenson. New York: Penguin Books, 1983.

Quackenbush, Robert. *Who Threw That Pie (The Birth of Movie Comedy)*. Chicago: Albert Whitman and Co., 1979.

Shannon, Michael J., Compiler. *Still More Jokes*. Chicago: Childrens Press, 1986.

Slubok, Shirley. *The Art of the Comic Strip*. New York: Macmillan Publishing Co., 1979.

Terban, Marvin. *In a Pickle and Other Funny Idioms*. Illus. Giulio Maestro. Boston: Clarion Books, 1981.

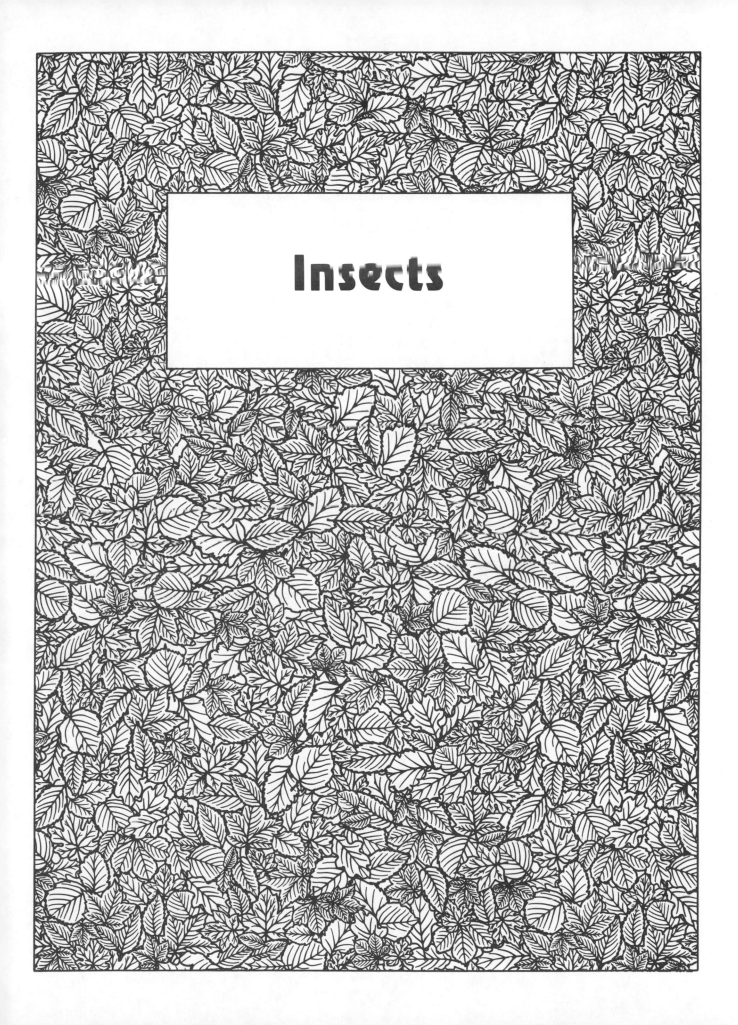

Insects

NOTES TO THE TEACHER

OBJECTIVES

To familiarize students with the general characteristics of insects.

To foster in-depth study of a few specific insects.

To familiarize students with the insects that inhabit their area.

MATERIALS

Pencils, crayons and/or markers, scissors, construction paper, staplers, glue, tape (optional), insect stickers, assorted materials for making insects (paper, tissue paper, tempera paint, dried beans, pebbles, nuts, clay, etc.), styrofoam trays or plastic plates, green tissue paper, white tissue paper, chenille stems (approximately 12" long), colored paper, insect collection bottles, magnifying glasses, soil, and grass seed (optional).

TOPIC OF THE WEEK

This introductory activity is to be used with the entire class as an introduction to the unit. To allow the students time to read and gather background information, it should be used a day or more before they go to Day's End Areas.

DAY'S END AREAS

Paper Crafts—Media Report Holder

The children will cut out and prepare beehives with pockets in which to keep completed Media Report Forms.

(Reproduce the beehive pattern on yellow paper.)

Media—Media Report Form

On these forms, the children will record information about the media materials that they have studied.

Research—Research Question Form

The children will choose particular insects to research. Questions they have asked about the insects and answers to those questions will be recorded on Research Question Forms.

(Reference materials and books about insects should be at the Day's End Area. Extra Research Question Forms should be provided. So that many different insects are being studied, provide a sign-up sheet on which the children will indicate the insects they have chosen to research.)

146

Writing—A Sticker Story

The children will each choose an insect from a sticker sheet, research that insect, write a story about the insect, and draw a picture that includes the chosen sticker.

Art—An Insect Zoo

The children will make insects from collected materials and place them in "habitats" created on plastic plates or styrofoam trays.

(If possible, read *The Insect Zoo* by Constance Ewbank to the children before they begin this activity. The children might bring their own plates and help collect the materials for making the insects [paper, tissue paper, tempera paints, various kinds of dried beans, pebbles, etc.]. If you wish, the children could plant grass seed in their plates several weeks ahead and keep records of its growth. Grass that gets too large can easily be clipped with scissors.)

Art—My Favorite Butterfly

The children will make tissue paper butterflies, mount them to form colored paper frames, and write descriptions of the butterflies they made.

Science—Observe and Record

The children will each gather information about an insect from their area, catch a specimen, and observe and record the insect's behavior at various times.

Spelling—My Spelling Book

The children will assemble books, the pages of which bear the names of insects. They then practice spelling the names. A blank page form on which the children may list other insects whose names they would like to learn to spell is also provided. (They may include these pages in their books, if desired.)

CULMINATING ACTIVITY

Have the children use the information they have gathered (pictures, facts, etc.) to write, prepare, and present an educational program. You might like them to use a format similar to educational programs they have seen on television. The program could be presented in their own classroom or for a larger group.

Name _____

TOPIC OF THE WEEK

Use the dictionary to find the meaning of the word *insect*. Write the meaning below.

_____

_____

_____

What words do you associate with the word *insect*?

_____   _____

_____   _____

_____   _____

_____   _____

_____   _____

Make a list of articles or stories about insects that are available to you from any media source (books, magazines, filmstrips, computer disks, tapes).

_____

_____

_____

_____

_____

_____

_____

_____

_____

_____

On the back of this sheet, make a list of insects in your area with which you are familiar.

Name _____

DAY'S END AREAS

PAPER CRAFTS

Materials

Crayons or markers, scissors, construction paper, stapler, glue, beehive pattern, bee pattern sheet(s), pencil, Media Report Form(s).

Activity

1. Cut out the beehive.

2. Cut a piece of construction paper in half lengthwise. Fold one half sheet of construction paper together and staple it on the sides.

3. Glue this pocket on the back of the beehive.

4. Color the bees correctly and cut them out. Fold the bees' wings upward on the dotted lines.

5. Choose titles from the list of media materials you made on the "Topic of the Week" sheet. Read, listen to, or view the material. Tape or glue a bee on your hive for each title you study.

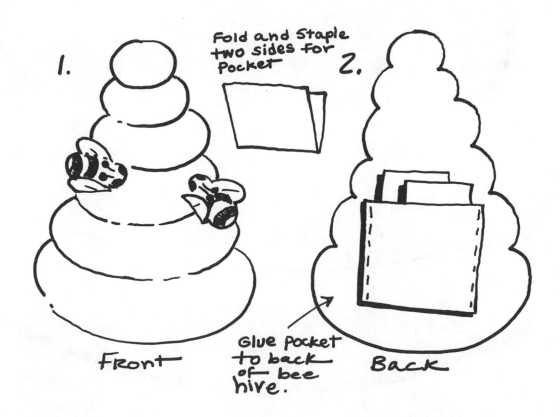

Glue Bees
to Hive For
each Title
read.

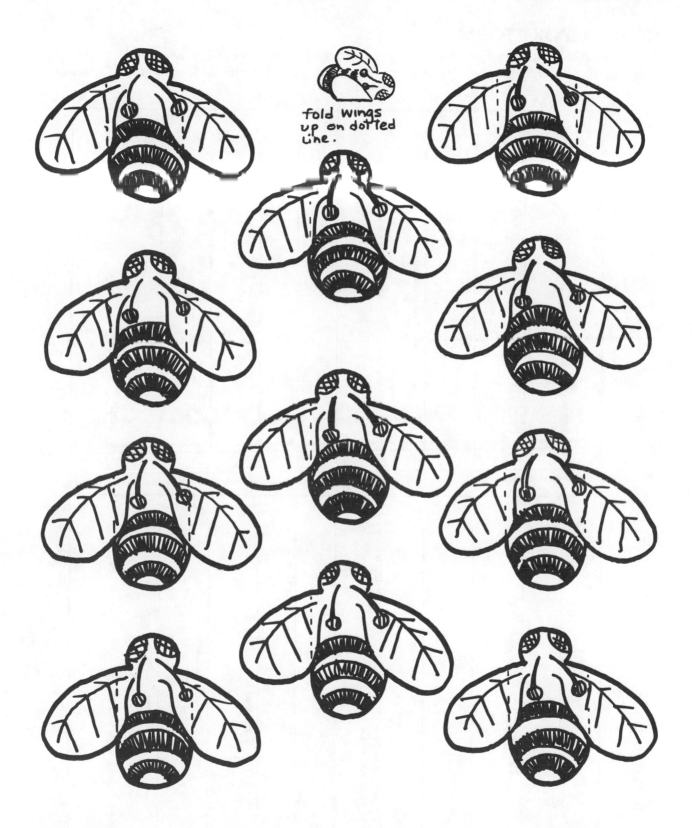

fold wings
up on dotted
line.

MEDIA REPORT FORM

For each item you read or hear, cut out and complete a report card. When you have finished your media report holder, place the completed cards in the holder. Use the back of the card for assignments.

My name is _____

Title of Book or Media Materials

Name of Author

Name of Illustrator

What did you discover in the material that was new to you?

My name is _____

Title of Book or Media Materials

Name of Author

Name of Illustrator

Comments:

My name is _____

Title of Book or Media Materials

Name of Author

Name of Illustrator

Write a paragraph or draw a picture of the most interesting part of what you studied.

My name is _____

Title of Book or Media Materials

Name of Author

Name of Illustrator

Briefly tell about what you studied.

RESEARCH QUESTION FORM

TOPIC: _____ RESEARCHER: _____

Questions that I would like to have answered by the research:

1. _____

? _____

3. _____

4. _____

5. _____

ANSWERS TO RESEARCH QUESTIONS

1. _____
_____
_____

2. _____
_____
_____

3. _____
_____
_____

4. _____
_____
_____

5. _____
_____
_____

References used: _____
_____

Name _____

CREATIVE WRITING

Materials
Insect stickers, crayons or markers, pencil.

Activity

1. Choose an insect from those shown on the sticker sheets that have been provided for you.

2. Gather information about that insect. Learn all you can about its habitat (where it lives), appearance (what it looks like), and behavior.

3. Think about what you have learned. Then write a story, real or imaginary, about the insect that you chose.

4. Use the space below and/or the back of this sheet to write your story and draw a picture about it. Include the sticker in your picture.

_____

_____

_____

_____

_____

_____

_____

_____

_____

_____

_____

_____

_____

_____

_____

Name _____

CREATIVE ART

Materials

Styrofoam trays or plastic plates, scissors, green tissue paper, glue, materials for making insects (paper, tissue paper, **paint**, **dried beans**, pebbles, nuts, clay, etc.)

Activity

1. Cut narrow strips from folded green tissue paper. Open them out and crush them with your fingers to make "grass." Fill a tray or plate with grass. A few drops of glue might help to hold it in place.

2. Using the materials the class has collected or those that are provided for you, create a number of insects. Use your imagination. Place the completed insects in the grass habitat.

3. Complete your zoo with any details you like. For example, twigs could become trees. Clay could become hills.

Name _____

MY FAVORITE BUTTERFLY

Materials
White tissue paper, chenille stems (approximately 12″ long), crayons or markers, scissors, glue, colored paper, white paper, pencil, yarn or string and paper punch (optional).

Activity
1. Using books, magazines, or other media sources, gather information about several butterflies. Then choose a specific butterfly you would like to make.

2. On the back of this sheet, sketch the butterfly you have chosen to make.

3. Fold a piece of tissue paper in half.

4. Cut out a butterfly (see illustration). Color the butterfly and add details with crayons or markers. If you are using markers, be sure to put a piece of paper behind your work so that the color will not get onto your desk or books.

5. Fold a 12″ chenille stem in half and twist it from the folded end upward as far as necessary to form the body of the butterfly.

6. Put a line of glue along the fold in the tissue butterfly. Lay the twisted body along the line of glue.

7. When the glue is dry, curl the top ends into antennae (see illustration).

8. Mount your butterfly on a piece of light-colored paper. Then glue that onto a larger piece of darker colored paper to form a frame.

9. You may, if you wish, punch holes at the top of the frame and tie a length of yarn or string through them to make a hanger (see illustration).

10. On another sheet of paper, write a description of, or a story or poem about, your butterfly. Glue it on the back of your framed butterfly.

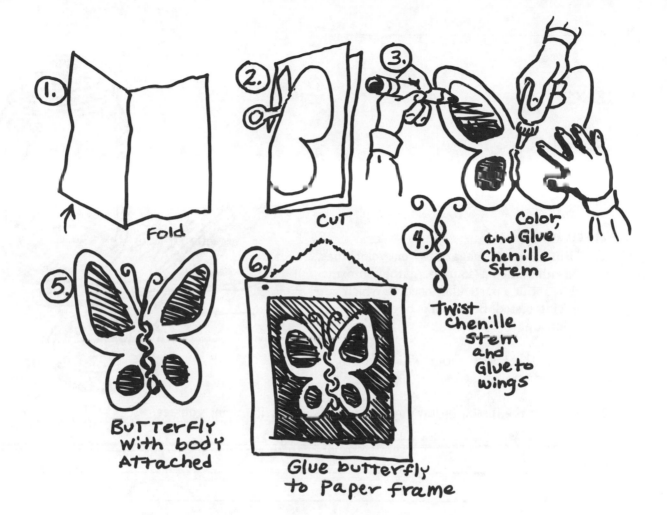

1. Fold

2. Cut

3.

4. Color, and Glue Chenille Stem

Twist chenille Stem and Glue to wings

5. Butterfly with body Attached

6. Glue butterfly to Paper frame

Name _____

SCIENCE

Materials
Insect collection bottle, magnifying glass, pencil.

Activity

1. Using books, magazines, encyclopedias, or other media sources, gather information about a particular insect in which you are interested. Be sure it is one that lives in your area.

2. Catch the insect about which you have studied.

3. Look at the insect with a magnifying glass. Describe what you see.

    _____

    _____

    _____

    _____

4. In the boxes below, record the time you observe the insect. Draw a picture of its behavior at that time. What is it doing? Repeat at other times for the remaining boxes.

(Use the back of this sheet, if necessary.)

Name _____

SPELLING

Materials
Scissors, spelling words sheet, stapler, pencil.

Activity

1. Cut out the book cover below and fold it on the dotted line. Write your name on the solid line.

2. Cut out the spelling words. Place them, evenly stacked, inside the cover and staple along the left edge to form a book.

3. Write each word (insect name) on the line below the printed name on the page.

4. Whenever you have time, practice spelling the words. You may look only at the picture on each page, spell the word, then check for correctness, or you may have a friend say the words for you to spell.

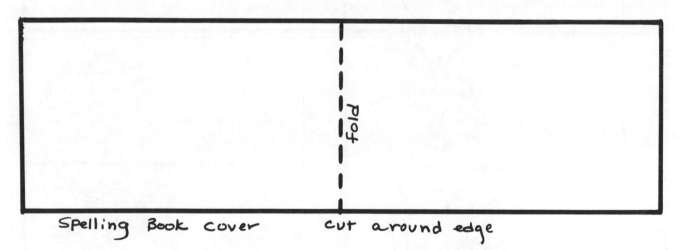

Spelling Book cover   cut around edge

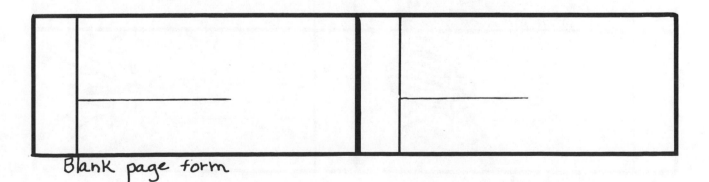

Blank page form

Grasshopper _____	Wasp _____
Praying Mantis _____	Cricket _____
Honey Bee _____	Moth _____
Lady Beetle _____	Firefly _____
Katydid _____	Housefly _____
Potato Beetle _____	Mosquito _____

BIBLIOGRAPHY

Cole, Joanna. *An Insect's Body*. Photos by Jerome Wexler and Raymond Mendez. New York: William Morrow and Co., 1984.

———. *Dragonflies*. Oxford Scientific Films. Photographs by George Bernard. New York: G. P. Putnam's Sons, 1980.

Danks, Hugh. *The Bug Book*. Illus. Joe Weissmann. New York: Workman Publishing, 1987.

Fischer-Nagel, Andreas, and Heiderose Fischer-Nagel. *Life of the Butterfly*. Minneapolis, Minn.: Carolrhoda Books, Inc., 1983.

———. *Life of the Honeybee*. Minneapolis, Minn.: Carolrhoda Books, Inc., 1986.

Hornblow, Leonora, and Arthur Hornblow. *Insects Do the Strangest Things*. Illus. Michael K. Frith. New York: Random House, 1968.

Horton, Casey. *Insects*. New York-Toronto: Gloucester Press, 1984.

Johnson, Sylvia A. *Chirping Insects*. Photos by Yuko Sato. Minneapolis, Minn.: Lerner Publications, 1986.

———. *Fireflies*. Photos by Satoshi Kuribayashi. Minneapolis, Minn.: Lerner Publications, 1986.

———. *Wasps*. Photographs by Hiroshi Ogawa. Minneapolis, Minn.: Lerner Publications, 1984.

Morris, Dean. *Insects That Live in Families*. Milwaukee, Wis.: MacDonald-Raintree, Inc., 1977.

Oda, Hidetomo. *Insect Hibernation*. Photos by Nanoa Kikaku. Milwaukee, Wis.: Raintree Publishers, 1986.

———. *Insects and Flowers*. Photos by Nanoa Kikaku. Milwaukee, Wis.: Raintree Publishers, 1986.

———. *Insects and Their Homes*. Milwaukee, Wis.: Raintree Publishers, 1986.

Overbeck, Cynthia. *Ants*. Photos by Satoshi Kuribayashi. Minneapolis, Minn.: Lerner Publications, 1982.

Patent, Dorothy Hinshaw. *Mosquitoes*. New York: Holiday, 1986.

Podendorf, Illa. *Insects*. Chicago: Childrens Press, 1981.

Porter, Keith. *Discovering Crickets and Grasshoppers*. Illus. Wendy Meadway. New York: Bookwright Press, 1986.

Islands

NOTES TO THE TEACHER

OBJECTIVES

To help students understand how islands are formed.

To familiarize students with a number of well-known islands and their locations.

MATERIALS

Tagboard or heavy paper (scraps are fine), scissors, glue, string, paper punches, plastic or foil plates, scraps of styrofoam (optional), pencils, crayons and markers, pockets (see Notes to the Teacher), thin, crisp paper cut into 8" squares, clay, construction paper.

TOPIC OF THE WEEK

This activity sheet is to be used as an introduction to the unit. To allow the students time to read and gather background information, it should be used a day or more before they go to Day's End Areas.

DAY'S END AREAS

Paper Crafts—Media Report Holder

The children will make paper suitcases in which to store media reports.

Media—Media Report Forms

The children will cut out travel tickets on which to record information about the media materials they have studied.

Clay—Create an Island

Using clay, the children will model island scenes in plastic or foil plates.

Art—An Island Scene

Each child will read a book about an island or one involving an island setting. Each student will then draw a picture of a scene from that book.

Art—Origami

The children will find, in any media, information about origami and will fold paper figures following instructions given in those materials.

(The paper they will use should be thin and crisp in texture and be cut into approximately 8" squares. *The New Book of Knowledge* [Grolier, Inc., Danbury, Conn.] provides good information and instructions for several figures.)

Social Studies—Where in the World Is It?

The children will cut out cards on which islands are named. The named islands will be located on maps or globes.

(Simple pockets for storing the cards can be provided by sealing plain, inexpensive envelopes and cutting across the width of the envelopes to form two pockets from each one.)

To give added familiarity with the locations of these islands, a group of three or four children might play a game with one set of cards. Place the cards in a container with a lid (small shoebox or a coffee can). Shake to mix up the cards. The students then take turns drawing a card. All the children in the game hunt for the named island. The one who finds it first may keep the card. The one with the most cards when all islands have been located will win that game.

1. Seal envelope

2. Cut envelope

3. Insert cards

Writing—A Travelogue

The children will write stories based on a picture with a travel theme.

Comprehension—Learn about Islands

The children will choose words from a given list to fill blank spaces in an article about islands.

CULMINATING ACTIVITY

Duplicate stationery forms (Sample Forms section) for the children. They may each decorate a sheet (or sheets) in keeping with the island theme. They may then pretend they are on islands somewhere and write letters to their parents or friends telling about their trips and adventures. They should mention such things as unusual sights and life forms. They should mention the languages that are spoken on the islands. Have them fold their letters and seal them with stickers or pieces of tape. On the other sides, they will address their letters and write return addresses from their island locations.

Name _____

TOPIC OF THE WEEK

Use the dictionary and write the definition of the word *island*.

_____
_____
_____
_____
_____

What words do you associate with the word *island*?

_____   _____
_____   _____
_____   _____
_____   _____
_____   _____
_____   _____

Make a list of any articles or stories about the topic that are available to you from any media source (books, magazines, filmstrips, computer disks, tapes).

_____
_____
_____
_____
_____
_____
_____
_____
_____
_____
_____
_____

Name _____

DAY'S END AREAS

PAPER CRAFTS

Materials
Scissors, glue, string, paper punch, suitcase pattern.

Activity
1. Cut out the suitcase pattern.

2. Fold on the dotted line. Glue along the sides.

3. Write your name and address on the tag below and cut it out. Punch a hole as shown.

4. Fold a 7″ piece of string in half and poke the folded end through the hole. Then slip the loose ends through the loop and pull up loosely. Tie the tag to the handle of your suitcase. People tag luggage in this manner so that their bags can be identified and to prevent loss.

5. You will use your suitcase to store Media Report Forms.

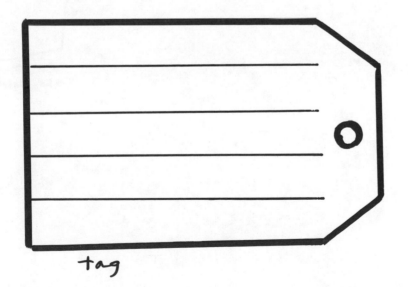

tag

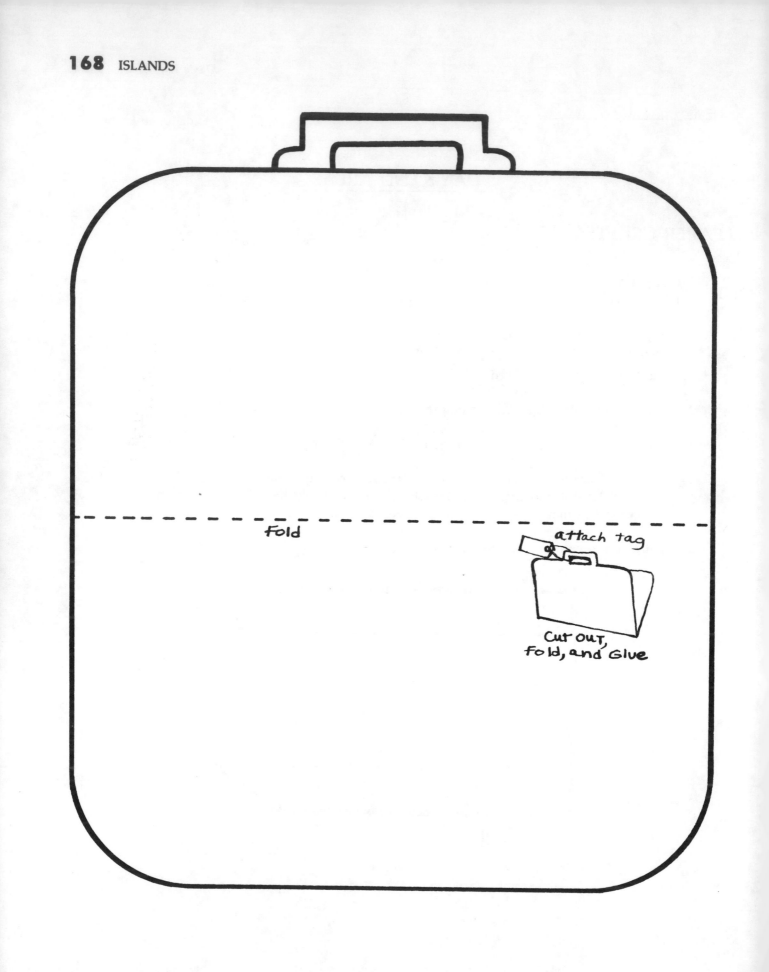

Fold

attach tag

Cut out,
fold, and Glue

Name _____

MEDIA REPORT FORM

Materials
Scissors, paper punch, pencil.

Activity

1. Choose a title from the list of media materials you made on the "Topic of the Week" sheet. Read, listen to, or view the material.

2. Cut out a ticket. Write the names of the author and illustrator of the material you studied.

3. Punch one box on the ticket for each ten pages you read. If you studied material from another media source, punch one box for each fifteen minutes you studied.

4. Place the completed ticket in your suitcase.

5. Prepare a ticket for each title you study.

my name _____

title _____

ILLustrator

ticket

Name _____

CLAY MODELING

Materials
Plastic or foil plate, scrap of styrofoam.

toothpick and
stick outrigger.
Foam boat.

Activity
1. Find and read a book about an island or a book that involves an island setting.

2. Now create an island, either the one you read about or an imaginary one. Use clay to build the island in the center of a plastic or foil plate.

3. Think carefully about what things you might see on the island. Create these details with clay.

4. When you are finished, put water in the plate to complete your island scene.

5. You might make a tiny boat from a bit of styrofoam and float it on the water.

6. In the space below, draw a picture of your island.

On the back of this page, write at least one paragraph to tell about the island you made.

Name _____

CREATIVE ART

Materials
Pencil, crayons and/or markers.

Activity
1. Read a book about an island or one that involves an island setting.
   Give the following information about the book:

   Title _____

   Author's Name _____

   Illustrator's Name _____

2. In the space below, draw a picture of a scene from the story. If you need more space, use the back of this page.

Name _____

ORIGAMI

Origami is an art in which figures are created by folding small squares of paper. The word means "paper folding" in the Japanese language. Origami probably began in China hundreds of years ago. Later, the art was brought to the island of Japan. The Japanese became famous for the beauty of the designs they folded. Today Japan has many very good origami artists.

Materials

Paper square(s).

Activity

1. Find at least one book or other source that contains information about origami and instructions for folding various figures.

2. Choose a design that you would like to make. Fold a paper square to create the figure.

3. Make as many different figures as you wish and have time to make.

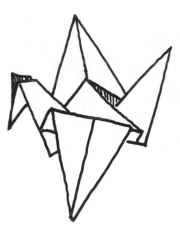

Name _____

SOCIAL STUDIES

Materials
Scissors, pocket, map or globe, card sheet.

Activity

1. On this and one other sheet, you will find cards with the names of some well-known islands. Cut the cards out.

2. Choose one card. On a map or globe, find the island named on the card. Each card has a picture of the continent which is nearest to that island or the name of the ocean where the island is located.

3. After you have located the island, place the card in a pocket.

4. Continue until you have located all the islands and placed all the cards in your pocket.

5. Make some other cards that relate to other islands. Then ask some other students to locate the islands that you have found.

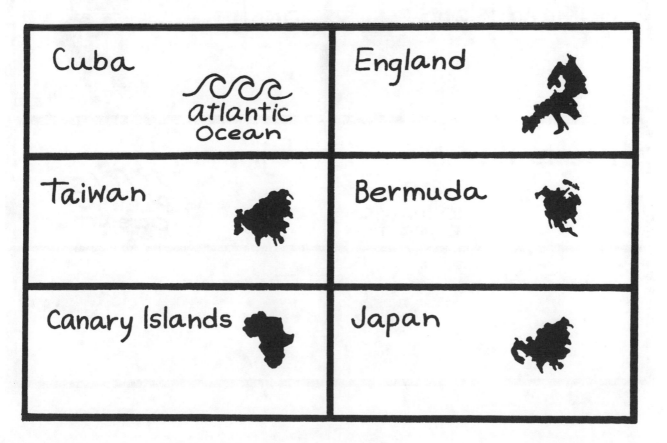

Hawaiian Islands

Pacific Ocean

Jamaica

atlantic Ocean

Madagascar

New Foundland

Cyprus

Galapagos Islands

Falkland Island

Sicily

Puerto Rico

atlantic Ocean

Fiji

Pacific Ocean

New Zealand

Tasmania

Name _____

CREATIVE WRITING

Materials
Pencil, lined paper.

Activity
1. Imagine that you have been on a long trip. Of what does the picture below remind you?

2. On the lines below the picture, write words that you think of as you look at the picture.

3. On another sheet of paper, write about your trip.

_____   _____

_____   _____

_____   _____

_____   _____

_____   _____

_____   _____

_____   _____

Name _____

COMPREHENSION

Materials
Pencil.

Activity
Read the article below carefully. Use the words from the list to fill the blank spaces. Be sure the words you choose fit the sense of the story. Use the dictionary, if necessary.

An island is a fascinating place to most of us. Many stories take place in island _____. But just what is an island? An island is _____ with _____ all around it, but it is _____ than a continent. An island can _____ in any body of water. Some are very _____, but new islands form all the _____.

There are four main ways in which islands come to be. Volcanoes under the sea _____ lava and rocks into the _____. Over time, as this _____, it builds up an area of land and becomes an island. Rivers and streams carry sand, silt, and gravel as they _____. When a river flows into a sea or lake, this material begins to build up little by little and becomes an island known as a barrier island.

Have you ever seen a piece of coral? It's beautiful and interestingly shaped. It is made of skeletons of tiny animals and dead plants. In shallow, _____ water, these can build and become _____ islands.

Some islands were once parts of continents, but because of the action of water or waves washing away dirt or the level of the sea rising, a part of the continent has become covered by water and separated from the rest of it. Sometimes pieces break apart and drift _____ and become islands.

Life on islands is varied. Continental islands usually have the same _____ and _____ life as the continents from which they came. The others start bare of _____. Some birds, animals, and insects swim or fly to them. Seeds _____ on water, and wind and birds _____ them. The plants and animals that live on islands often evolve (change because of conditions) and hardly resemble those in other _____. Some grow very _____ or lose size. Some insects and animals lose abilities they once had.

So you see, islands are beautiful, strange, and wonderful places.

large	places	form
land	time	smaller
carry	warm	spew
air	plant	coral
move	they	life
water	old	away
animal	settings	float
		settles

Answer key on p. 179.

BIBLIOGRAPHY

Andersen, Madelyn Klein. *Greenland: Island at the Top of the World*. New York: Dodd, Mead & Co., 1983.

Baker, Eleanor Z. *New Zealand Today*. Austin, Tex.: Steck-Vaughn Co., 1972.

Ball, John, and Chris Fairclough. *Let's Visit Fiji*. Bridgeport, Conn.: Burke Publishing Co., 1985.

_____. *We Live in New Zealand*. Photography by Chris Fairclough. New York: Bookwright Press, 1982.

Bruns, Roger A., and Haldon K. Richardson. *Bermuda*. Edgemont, Penn.: Chelsea House Publishers, 1986.

Burns, Geoff. *Take a Trip to New Zealand*. Ed. Henry Pluckrose. New York: Franklin Watts, 1983.

Carpenter, Allan. *Hawaii*. Chicago: Childrens Press, 1979.

Fairclough, Chris. *We Live in Ireland*. New York: Bookwright, 1986.

Fradin, Dennis. *Hawaii: In Words and Pictures*. Chicago: Childrens Press, 1980.

Griffiths, John. *Let's Visit Cuba*. Bridgeport, Conn.: Burke Publishing Co., 1983.

Hassall, S., and P. J. Hassall. *Let's Visit Bahrain*. Bridgeport, Conn.: Burke Publishing Co., 1985.

Holland, Isabelle. *The Island*. Boston: Little, Brown and Co., 1984.

Hubley, John, and Penny Hubley. *A Family in Jamaica*. Minneapolis, Minn.: Lerner Publications Co., 1985.

Jacobsen, Peter Otto, and Preben Sejer Kristensen. *A Family in Japan*. New York: Bookwright Press, 1986.

_____. *Japan*. Chicago: Childrens Press, 1982.

Lye, Keith. *Take a Trip to Philippines*. London: Franklin Watts Ltd., 1985.

McCulla, Patricia. *Bahamas*. New York/New Haven/Philadelphia: Chelsea House Publishers, 1988.

Newfoundland. Agincourt, Ontario: GLC/Silver Burdett Publishers, 1984.

Nova Scotia. Agincourt, Ontario: GLC/Silver Burdett Publishers, 1984.

O'Dell, Scott. *Island of the Blue Dolphins*. Boston: Houghton Mifflin, 1960.

Prince Edward Island. Agincourt, Ontario: GLC/Silver Burdett Publishers, 1984.

Rydell, Wendy. *All about Islands*. Illus. Ray Burns. Mahwah, N.J.: Troll Associates, 1984.

St. John, Jetty. *A Family in England*. Minneapolis, Minn.: Lerner Publications, 1988.

Scott, Jack Denton, and Ozzie Sweet. *Islands of Wild Horses*. New York: G. P. Putnam's Sons, 1978.

Stevens, Rita. *Madagascar*. New York/New Haven/Philadelphia: Chelsea House Publishers, 1988.

Thomas, Ruth, and Neil Thomas. *A Family in Thailand*. Minneapolis, Minn.: Lerner Publications, 1988.

Winslow, Zachery. *Puerto Rico*. Edgemont, Penn.: Chelsea House, 1986.

ANSWER KEY

COMPREHENSION

settings

land

water

smaller

form

old

time

spew

air

settles

move

warm

coral

away

plant

animal

life

float

carry

places

large

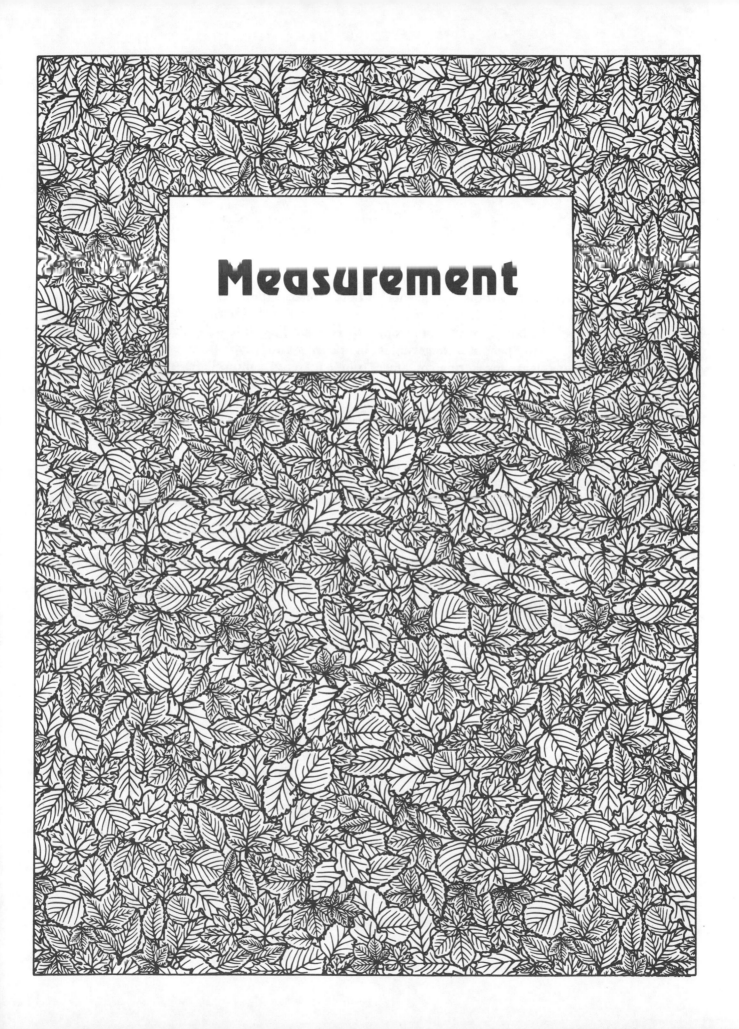

Measurement

NOTES TO THE TEACHER

OBJECTIVES

To give students basic knowledge of standard and metric measurement.

To help students learn to apply this knowledge in everyday situations.

MATERIALS

Tape measures (standard and metric), rulers (standard and metric), yardsticks and meter sticks (optional), pencils, clay, scales (standard and metric), various boxes in different sizes, crayons or colored pencils, plastic sandwich bags, measuring cups and spoons (standard and metric), small mixing containers, stirring tools, ingredients for Popzel Snacks (popcorn, pretzel sticks, Chex cereal, peanuts [optional], butter flavored oil, Hidden Valley Ranch Original Party Dip Mix, garlic powder), bowls for mixing, spoons for mixing, waxed paper, paper towels, ingredients for Peanutty Popcorn Balls (crunchy peanut butter, vanilla, light corn syrup, dry milk, popcorn, chocolate chips [optional]), water, large measuring containers (pint, quart, ½ gallon, liter), sinks or pans.

TOPIC OF THE WEEK

This introductory activity is to be used with the class as a whole as an introduction to the unit. To allow the students time to read and gather information, it should be used a day or more before they go to Day's End Areas.

DAY'S END AREAS

Length—Standard
Length—Metric

The children will measure a number of common objects to determine widths, lengths, heights, circumferences, and perimeters of the objects.

Weight—Standard
Weight—Metric

To gain familiarity with the use of scales and with various weights, the children will weigh clay. They will estimate weights of objects and then weigh them to determine actual weights.

(You might like to make up additional problems at your students' level that use all four math operations [+, −, ÷, ×]. Example: Weigh 2 ounces of clay and 6 ounces of clay. What is the total number of ounces?)

Area and Volume—Standard
Area and Volume—Metric

The students will measure various objects and compute the areas of the surfaces and the volumes of the objects. They will create graph paper designs and determine the areas of the designs.
(You will need to have several boxes of assorted sizes for the children to measure.)

Liquid Measurement—Standard
Liquid Measurement Metric

The students will measure water into larger containers to learn the concept of capacity and the facts of equivalency.

Measuring Ingredients—Standard
Measuring Ingredients—Metric

The students will apply their knowledge of measurement by using recipes to make snacks. They will use both standard and metric measurements.

Two students can work together making Popzel Snacks as the recipe makes enough oil dressing for two bags of snacks. You might also want to show the students how to hold the bags closed and knead the contents to distribute the oil.

Provide small plastic or paper cups for mixing the dressing and stirring tools such as clean popsicle sticks or plastic stirrers.

You will want to provide popped popcorn. One quart will make sixteen bags of snacks. You will need to adjust amounts of ingredients according to your class size. Pretzels should be small, about 2", sticks. They measure better if they are broken into 1" pieces. You might want to break them ahead of time. Any kind of Chex cereal works well.

Plastic whipped topping containers would make suitably sized bowls for mixing Peanutty Popcorn Balls. The students might bring their own. Chocolate chips (30 ml) may be added to this recipe, if desired.

CULMINATING ACTIVITY

You might want the students to do the Make a Snack activities as a culminating activity. Serving a simple drink with the food would create a sort of party atmosphere.

You might also provide an assortment of cookbooks and 4" x 6" cards, let them each choose a recipe that they think they would enjoy, and have them copy the recipes onto the cards to take home. Check the recipes for accuracy in copying.

The students might create designs using only lines made from rulers for a creative art project.

Name _____

TOPIC OF THE WEEK

    People often need to know how large something is or how far away it is. Sometimes they need to know how much a container will hold or how much there is of some commodity (any thing that is bought or sold). Finding out facts such as these is called measurement.

Use a dictionary to discover and write the meanings of the words below as they are related to measurement.

Length _____

_____

Volume _____

_____

Weight (mass) _____

_____

Capacity _____

_____

List below the names of any media materials on the topic of measurement that you have read, listened to, or viewed.

_____

_____

_____

_____

_____

_____

_____

_____

_____

_____

Name _____

DAY'S END AREAS

LENGTH (Inches, feet, yards)

Materials
Tape measure, ruler, yardstick (optional), pencil.

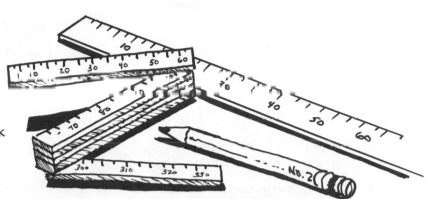

Activity
1. Study the following definitions:
    a. The perimeter is the distance around any shape other than a circle (add the length of all sides).
    b. The circumference is the distance around a circle or anything that is round in shape.
    c. An estimate is a judgement or an opinion (your guess) as to size, length, distance, etc.

2. Measure the things listed below and fill in the chart. Indicate whether the measurement is in inches, feet, or yards.

3. Choose other objects to measure, and list them on the blank lines in the chart.

OBJECT	ESTIMATE	ACTUAL MEASUREMENT
Length of a shelf in your room		
Width of a table in the room		
Height of a table in the room		
Length of a bulletin board		
Height of a wastepaper basket		
Circumference of a (round) basket		
Perimeter of your desk top		

Name _____

LENGTH (Centimeters, meters)

Materials

Metric tape measure, metric ruler and/or meter stick, pencil.

Activity

1. Study the following definitions:

    a. The perimeter is the distance around any shape other than a circle (add the length of all sides).

    b. The circumference is the distance around a circle or anything that is round in shape.

    c. An estimate is a judgement or an opinion (your guess) as to size, length, distance, etc.

2. Measure the things listed below and fill in the chart. Indicate whether the measurement is in centimeters (cm) or meters (m).

3. Choose other objects to measure, and list them on the blank lines in the chart.

OBJECT	ESTIMATE	ACTUAL MEASUREMENT
Length of a shelf in your room		
Width of a table in the room		
Height of a table in the room		
Length of a bulletin board		
Height of a wastepaper basket		
Circumference of a (round) basket		
Perimeter of your desk top		

Name _____

WEIGHT (MASS)
Pounds, ounces

Materials
Clay, standard scale, pencil.

Activity
1. Weigh portions of clay as instructed below and fill in the blanks.

   a. Weigh enough clay to make sixteen ounces.

   b. Weigh enough clay to make one pound.
      A pound is _____ ounces.

   c. Weigh enough clay to make one-fourth pound.
      One-fourth pound is _____ ounces.

   d. Weigh enough clay to make one ounce.

   e. Weigh enough clay to make two ounces.

   f. Weigh enough clay to make one-half pound.

   g. Weigh enough clay to make eight ounces.
      One-half pound is _____ ounces.

2. An estimate is a judgement or an opinion (your guess) as to size, weight, length, etc.

3. Choose some objects in the area and estimate their weights. Then weigh them and fill in the chart below. Be sure to indicate whether the weights are in pounds or ounces.

OBJECT	ESTIMATE	ACTUAL WEIGHT

Name _____

WEIGHT (MASS)
Grams, kilograms

Materials
Clay, metric scale, pencil.

Activity

1. Weigh portions of clay as instructed below and fill in the blanks.

    a. Weigh enough clay to make one-half kilogram.
        One-half kilogram is _____ grams.
        One kilogram is _____ grams.
        (If your scale does not weigh this large a number of grams, use a dictionary or encyclopedia to find this information.)
    b. Weigh enough clay to make one gram.
    c. Weigh enough clay to make 10 grams.
    d. Weigh enough clay to make 20 grams.
    e. Weigh enough clay to make 100 grams.
    f. Weigh enough clay to make 200 grams.

2. An estimate is a judgement or an opinion (your guess) as to size, weight, length, etc.

3. Choose some objects in the area and estimate their weights. Then weigh them and fill in the chart below.

OBJECT	ESTIMATE	ACTUAL WEIGHT

Name _____

AREA AND VOLUME—Standard

Area and volume are measured in inches, feet, or yards depending on the size of the object or space. Area refers to the amount of space on a flat surface. To find the area of a square or rectangular surface, you must measure to determine its length and width. Then multiply the two figures.

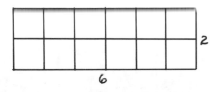

6″ x 2″ = 12 square inches

Volume refers to the amount of space within a three dimensional figure such as a box. To determine the volume, you must measure to find the length, width, and height of the figure. You then multiply length x width x height to determine volume in cubic inches, feet or yards.

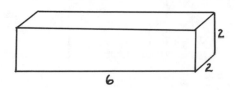

6 x 2 x 2 = 24 cubic inches (You could stack this many 1″ blocks inside the box.)

Materials

Ruler and/or tape measure, boxes, 1″ graph paper, crayons or colored pencils, pencil.

Activity

1. Measure the length and width of the top of your desk and determine the area of the surface. _____ square inches

2. Measure and determine the area of a table in the room. _____ square _____

3. Measure at least three boxes which your teacher will provide for you and figure the volume of each one. Measure in inches, feet, or yards depending on the size of each box.

4. Choose three colors with which to make a design on 1″ graph paper. Completely color in squares to create your design.

5. When your design is complete, supply the following information (count the squares of each color).
    a. I have _____ square inches of _____.
    　　　　　　　　　　　　　　　　　　　　　　　　　(color)
    b. I have _____ square inches of _____.
    　　　　　　　　　　　　　　　　　　　　　　　　　(color)
    c. I have _____ square inches of _____.
    　　　　　　　　　　　　　　　　　　　　　　　　　(color)

SQUARE INCHES

Name _____

AREA AND VOLUME—Metric

Area and volume are measured in centimeters or meters depending on the size of the object or space. Area refers to the amount of space on a flat surface. To find the area of a square or rectangular surface, you must measure to determine its length and width. Then multiply the two figures.

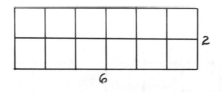

2 cm x 6 cm = 12 square cm

Volume refers to the amount of space within a three dimensional figure such as a box. To determine the volume, you must measure to find the length, width, and height of the figure. You then multiply length x width x height to determine volume in cubic centimeters or meters.

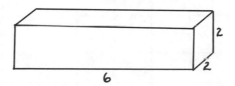

2 cm x 2 cm x 6 cm = 24 cubic centimeters (You could stack this many 1 cm blocks inside the box.)

Materials
Metric ruler and/or tape measure, boxes, 1 cm graph paper, crayons or colored pencils, pencil.

Activity
1. Measure the length and width of the top of your desk and determine the area of the surface. _____ square centimeters

2. Measure and determine the area of a table in the room. _____ square _____

3. Measure at least three boxes which your teacher will provide for you and figure the volume of each one. Measure in centimeters or meters depending on the size of each box.

4. Choose three colors with which to make a design on 1 cm graph paper. Completely color in squares to create your design.

5. When your design is complete, supply the following information (count the squares of each color).
   a. I have _____ square centimeters of _____.
                                                           (color)
   b. I have _____ square centimeters of _____.
                                                           (color)
   c. I have _____ square centimeters of _____.
                                                           (color)

SQUARE CENTIMETERS

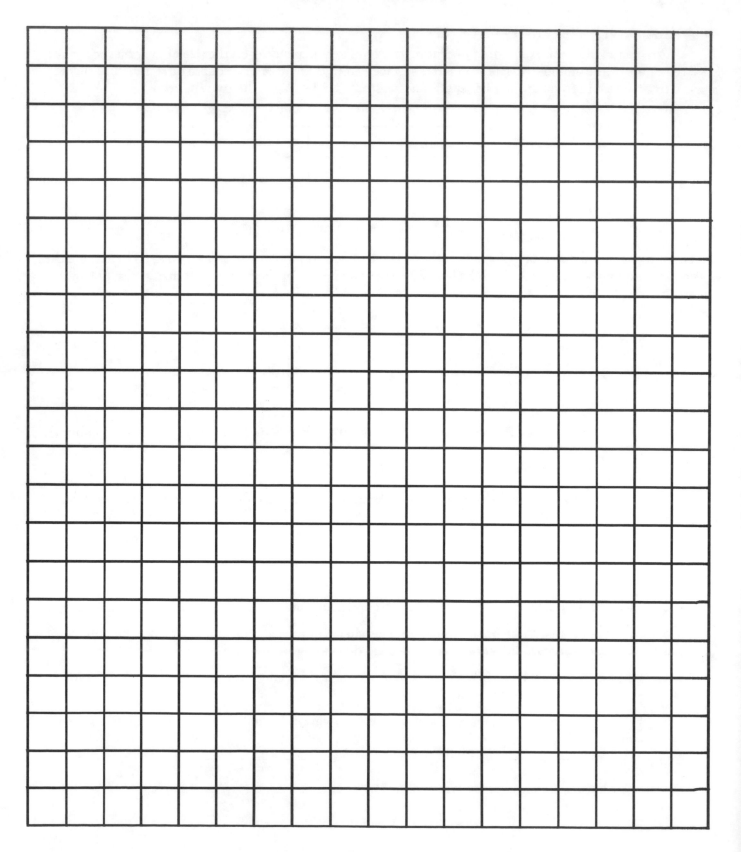

Name _____

LIQUID MEASUREMENT—Standard

Materials
Water, a measuring cup or a set of measuring cups
that show ounces, measuring spoons, measuring
containers in pint, quart, and half gallon sizes, pencil.

Activity
To determine the facts needed to fill the blanks in the following statements, use the smaller container
to fill the larger one with water. Work carefully and fill all the measuring containers accurately to the
correct levels.

1. How many cups are in one pint? _____

2. How many cups are in one quart? _____

3. How many cups are in a half gallon? _____

4. How many ounces does it take to make one cup? _____

5. How many ½ cups does it take to make one cup? _____

6. How many ⅓ cups does it take to make one cup? _____

7. How many tablespoons does it take to make ¼ cup? _____

8. How many tablespoons does it take to make ⅓ cup? _____

9. How many teaspoons does it take to make 1 tablespoon? _____

10. How many ¼ teaspoons does it take to make one teaspoon? _____

Name _____

LIQUID MEASUREMENT—Metric

Materials
Water, pencil, metric measuring cups and spoons, liter sized measuring container, sink or pan.

Activity

1. To determine the facts needed to fill the blanks in the following statements, study the measuring containers that your teacher provides. Notice the numbers shown on the containers.
    a. There are _____ milliliters (ml) in a liter (l).
    b. Use the dictionary to learn the meaning of the prefix *deci*. Write the meaning below.

        _____

        (If you had an apple cut into ten equal pieces, one of those pieces would be one-tenth of the apple.)
    c. There are _____ deciliters (dl) in one liter.

2. Practice measuring amounts of liquid (water) as instructed below. Pour the water into a sink or pan as your teacher directs.
    a. Measure 100 ml of water.
        One hundred ml = _____ deciliter(s).
    b. Measure 150 ml of water.
    c. Measure 250 ml of water.
        250 ml = _____ of a liter.
    d. A decimal (.) before a number means tenths. Thus .5 = 5/10 (five of ten pieces of the apple).
        250 ml = _____ deciliters
    e. Measure 500 ml of water.
        500 ml = _____ deciliters
    f. Measure one l of water.

3. You are given a list of things below. Write ml (milliliter), l (liter), or dl (deciliter) to show which would be the best measure to use for each. (Some things may be measured in ml or dl.)
    a. Gasoline to fill a car _____
    b. Milk for a pudding _____
    c. Vanilla for a cake _____
    d. Juice for a baby bottle _____
    e. Water to fill a car radiator _____
    f. Cinnamon for cookies _____
    g. Butter to fry an egg _____
    h. Flour for pancakes _____
    i. Water to fill a bathtub _____

Answer key on page 198.

Name _____

MEASURING INGREDIENTS
Standard

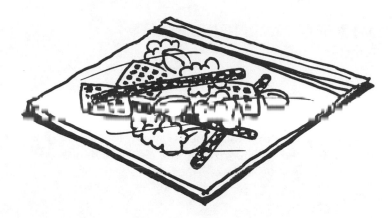

Materials
Plastic sandwich bag, ingredients which your teacher will supply, measuring cups and spoons, small container, stirring tool.

Activity
1. Be sure that your hands and work area are clean.

2. Follow the recipe below to make a snack that you will enjoy.

Popzel Snack

Ingredients

1/2 cup unsalted popcorn	2 teaspoons butter flavored oil
1/4 cup pretzel sticks	1/2 teaspoon Hidden Valley Ranch
1/3 cup Chex cereal	Original Party Dip mix
2 tablespoons peanuts (optional)	1/8 teaspoon garlic powder

Measure the popcorn, pretzels, cereal, and peanuts and pour them into a sandwich bag.

In the small container, combine the oil, dip mix, and garlic powder and stir well. Keep it well stirred and measure one teaspoon of the oil mixture. Pour it over the ingredients in the bag. Hold the top of the bag tightly shut. Shake and gently knead the bag to coat the snacks evenly with the oil mixture.

Name _____

MEASURING INGREDIENTS
Metric

Materials
Bowl, ingredients which your teacher will provide, metric measuring cups and spoons, spoon for mixing, piece of waxed paper, damp paper towel for cleaning hands.

Activity
1.   Be sure your hands and work area are clean.

2.   Follow the recipe below to make a snack that you will enjoy.

Peanutty Popcorn Balls

Ingredients

30 ml crunchy peanut butter	60 ml dry milk
	120 ml popcorn
6 ml vanilla	30 ml light corn syrup

In the bowl, combine the crunchy peanut butter, vanilla and corn syrup. Mix well. Add the popcorn.

Stir and fold gently until the popcorn is coated with the peanut butter mixture. Add the dry milk. Stir and fold until the milk is thoroughly mixed with the peanut mixture. The mixture will be stiff, but keep stirring and folding until all the dry milk is mixed in.

With your hands, roll bits of the mixture into 1" balls and place the balls on a piece of waxed paper. Makes 7-8 (1") balls.

BIBLIOGRAPHY

Ardley, Neil. *Making Metric Measurements (Action Series)*. New York: Franklin Watts, 1983.

Baird, Eva-Lee, and Rose Wyler. *Going Metric the Fun Way*. Illus. Talwaldis Stubis. New York: Doubleday & Co., 1980.

Bitter, Gary G., and Thomas H. Metos. *Exploring with Metrics*. New York: Julian Messner, 1975.

Branley, Franklyn M. *Measure with Metric*. Illus. Loretta Lustig. New York: Thomas Y. Crowell, 1975.

_____. *Think Metric*. New York: Thomas Y. Crowell Co., 1972.

Foster, Leslie. *Rand McNally Mathematics Encyclopedia*. Chicago: Rand McNally, 1985.

Holl, Adelaide, and Seymour Reit. *Time and Measuring*. Illus. Harry McNaught. New York: Western Publishing Co., Inc., 1970.

Nentl, Jerolyn Ann. *The Gram Is*. Mankato, Minn.: Crestwood House, 1976.

_____. *The Liter Is*. Mankato, Minn.: Crestwood House, 1976.

_____. *The Meter Is*. Mankato, Minn.: Crestwood House, 1976.

Podendorf, Illa. *How Big Is a Stick?* Illus. Richard Mlodock. Chicago: Childrens Press, 1971.

Russell, Solveig Paulson. *Size, Distance, Weight: A First Look at Measuring*. Illus. Margot Tomes. New York: Henry Z. Walck, Inc., 1968.

Srivastava, Jane Jonas. *Weighing and Measuring*. Illus. Aliti. New York: Thomas Y. Crowell, 1970.

Thomas, Annabel. *Weighing and Measuring*. Illus. Graham Round. Chicago: Childrens Press, 1986.

ANSWER KEY

LIQUID MEASUREMENT (Metric)

1. a. 1000
   b. one tenth of
   c. 10

2. a. l
   b. —
   c. ¼
   d. 2.5
   e. 5
   f. —

3. a. l
   b. dl or ml
   c. ml
   d. ml or dl
   e. l
   f. ml
   g. ml
   h. dl or ml
   i. l

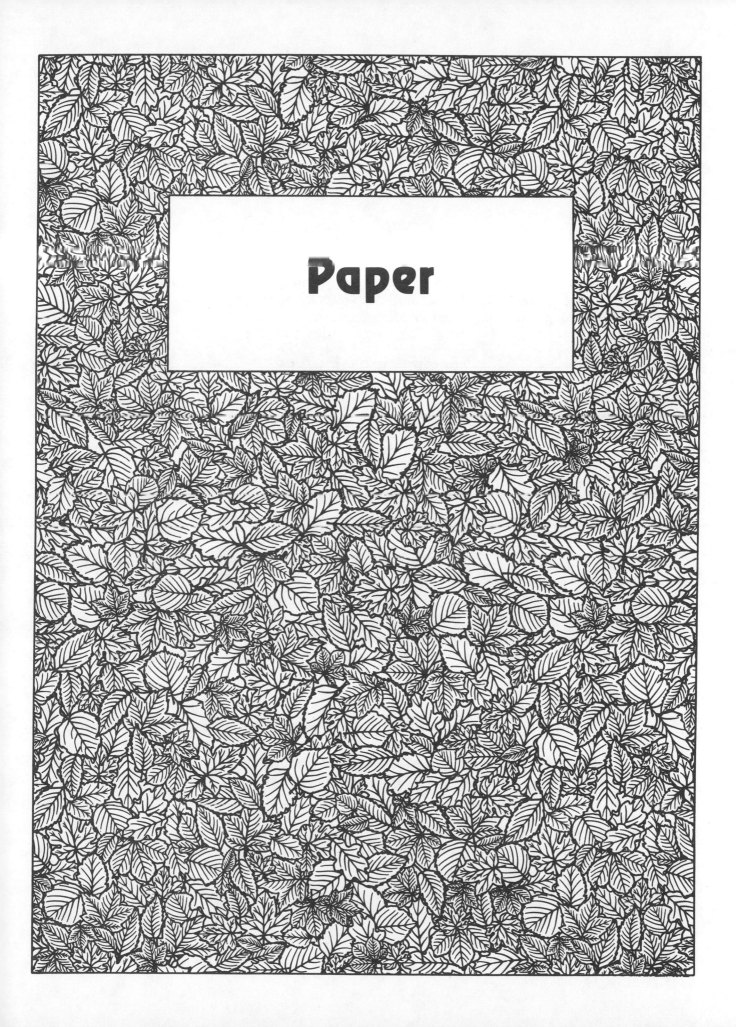

Paper

NOTES TO THE TEACHER

OBJECTIVES

To increase students' awareness of the importance and uses of paper in their everyday lives.

To help students understand how paper is made.

To foster responsibility in the use of paper and proper disposal of waste paper.

MATERIALS

Pieces of sturdy, light colored cloth (10" x 14" for each child), scissors, light rope or heavy cord, crayons, markers, large-eyed needles, white thread, white paper, pencils, glue, many kinds and textures of paper, magnifying glasses, small containers for water, water, construction paper, plain paper bags (medium size), paper punch, reinforcements.

TOPIC OF THE WEEK

This introductory activity is to be used as an introduction to the unit. To allow the students time to read and gather background information, it should be used a day or more before they go to the Day's End Areas. You will need to read to the children an article from an encyclopedia or other source from which they can discover the information needed for the first part of the activity.

DAY'S END AREAS

The children take task sheets, collect the necessary materials, and go to designated areas to work.

Fabric Crafts—Media Report Holder

The children will make replicas of a newspaper carrier's bag in which to store Media Report forms. (The children might bring their own pieces of cloth for this activity.)

Media—Media Report Form

On sample newspaper pages, the children will write reviews of media materials they've listened to, read, or viewed.

(You might want to explain what a column is and look at some newspapers. You might also suggest that the children clip sheets of lined paper behind "Media News" to make it easier to write neatly.)

Research—From Tree to Paper

The children will research the process of making paper. They will write the steps in the process in correct order on the tree trunks.

(Reproduce the trunks on light brown paper.)

Research—Collage Tree Top

The children will tear pieces from many kinds and textures of paper and use them to create tree tops in collage.

Science—Let's See

The children will tear many kinds of paper, observe the fibers with magnifying glasses, and record their observations.

Paper Crafts—Paper Folding

The children will fold paper into interesting objects.

Art—Torn Paper Designs

The children will create designs or pictures using only torn paper and glue.

Social Studies—A Personal Litterbag

The children will make litterbags for use at school or home.

CULMINATING ACTIVITY

Have each child bring a paper bag (decorated, if desired) containing something made of paper. In turn, the children will hold up their sacks. In an attempt to identify an object, the other children may ask questions that can be answered *yes* or *no*. Occasionally a more specific answer may have to be given. Continue until all objects have been identified.

You might like to discuss *conservation* with your students. If there is a nearby paper collection station, you might have a paper collection project.

Write a class newspaper to send home to parents.

Name _____

TOPIC OF THE WEEK

Listen carefully to the article your teacher will read to you to discover two things from which paper can be made.

_____   _____

Make a list of all the ways you can think of that paper is used in the world today.

_____   _____
_____   _____
_____   _____
_____   _____
_____   _____
_____   _____
_____   _____

Make a list of any articles or stories about the topic that are available to you from any media source (books, magazines, filmstrips, computer disks, tapes).

_____
_____
_____
_____
_____
_____
_____
_____
_____

Name _____

DAY'S END AREAS

FABRIC CRAFTS—Let's Make a Newspaper Bag

Newspaper delivery people usually have special cloth bags in which to carry the papers.

Materials

Sturdy (light-colored) 10″ x 14″ piece of cloth, scissors, light rope or heavy cord (20″), markers, large-eyed needle, white thread, scrap paper.

Activity

1. Fold ½″ hems on each narrow end of the cloth and sew them. Make several stitches on top of each other to fasten the thread at the ends.

2. Fold the cloth so that the hems are at the top, the raw edges inside. Place a piece of scrap paper inside. Using a permanent marker, write the name of your "newspaper" (Media News) on the front of the bag. Try to make it look as much like the name on the paper as possible.

3. Now fold the cloth so that the writing is inside and the raw hem edges are outside. Make a knot close to each end of the cord. Lay the cord inside the bag with the knots beyond the edges of the cloth (see illustration). Stitch down each side. Stitch through the cord.

4. Turn your bag right side out.

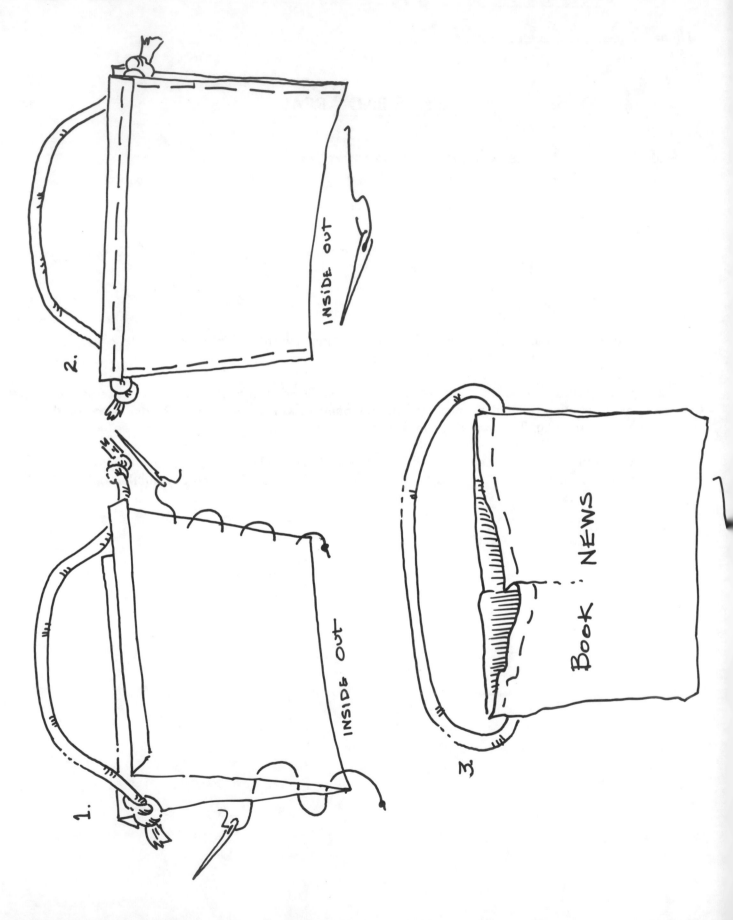

Name _____

MEDIA REPORT FORM—Media Reviews

Newspapers and magazines often print reviews of books, plays, television programs, and movies. A review is written by someone who has seen or attended an event or read a book or other printed material. The reviewer briefly tells about the experience or story: where and when it happened, who was involved, what happened. Then the reviewer states an opinion of the worth of the material or performance and tells why it is good or bad.

Materials

Pencil, lined paper, sample newspaper page.

Activity

1. Choose a title from the list you made on the "Topic of the Week" sheet. Read, listen to, or view the material.

2. You are given a blank newspaper page. Fill in the line below the title with your town, state, day, month, and year of "publication" (see illustration).

3. You will be writing a review of the material you studied. You might want to do this on another sheet of paper and copy it neatly onto the newspaper page after you've edited your work. Most newspaper stories have datelines at the beginning. A dateline tells where the event happened or where the story took place. Write the location first if it is stated (see illustration).

4. Complete your review by briefly summarizing what you studied and then telling if you thought it was good or bad. Was it interesting? Well written? Nicely illustrated? Be sure to give reasons for your opinion.

5. Write a headline for your review. A headline is in larger print than the rest of the story and gives an idea of the content of the story. Make your headline interesting so others will want to read your review.

6. For each title you study, write a review and a headline. Use as many newspaper pages as you need. When you have finished a page, fold it in half, print side out. Place it in your newspaper bag.

MEDIA NEWS

Tipton, Utah   Sunday, June 6, 1988   VOL. 1

(Headline)   ISLAND ADVENTURE

(Dateline) Padre Island, Tex.- On a hot

day in the Gulf of Mexico, a

Name _____

RESEARCH—From Tree to Paper

Materials
Pencil, tree trunk pattern, scissors, glue.

Activity

1. You probably already know that most paper began as a tree in a forest. You are given a list of things that must happen for a tree to become paper. Use a book or encyclopedia to learn the order in which these things happen.

2. Write the steps in the correct order on the tree trunk.

3. Cut out the trunk and put it aside until you have completed a collage tree top.

The chips are cooked.

The pulp is pressed into sheets.

The wood is cut into chips.

The paper is dried.

The bark is removed.

The paper is wound into huge rolls.

The cooked pulp is drained and washed.

Trees are sawed in the forest.

Answer key on page 217.

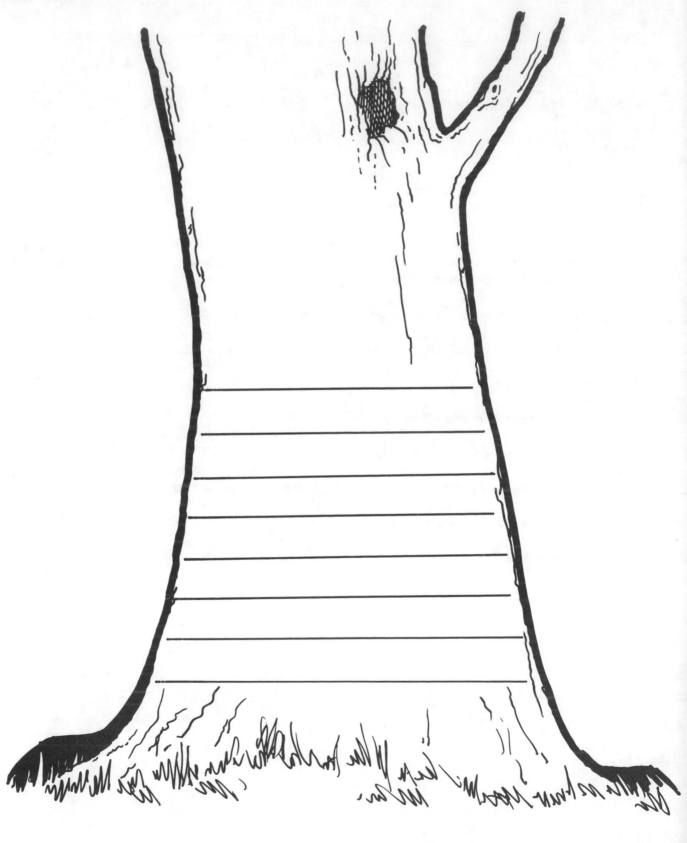

COLLAGE TREE TOP

Materials

Various kinds of paper, scissors, glue.

Activity

1. Cut out the tree top shape on this page.

2. Find as many different kinds of paper as you can. Cut pieces of paper and glue them onto the tree top to cover it completely. The more kinds and textures you use, the nicer your tree will be.

3. Glue the tree top to the trunk.

Name _____

SCIENCE—Let's See

Materials

A variety of different kinds of paper, magnifying glass, pencil, small containers for water, water, white paper.

Activity

1. Tear pieces from different kinds of paper. Use a magnifying glass to observe the fibers along the torn edges.

2. Put pieces of paper into water and observe what happens. Do they fade? Do they stretch? Record your observations on the chart below. If you need more room, use the back of this sheet.

Kind of paper	Record your observations

3. Some kinds of paper bleed (color runs) when they are wet. Try painting a picture with wet pieces of these kinds of papers.

Name _____

PAPER CRAFTS—Paper Folding

Paper has long been used as an art medium. People draw and paint on it. They cut it into fancy designs. They fold it to create interesting shapes and objects.

Materials

Scissors, paper folding pattern sheet, white paper, construction paper, pencils, crayons or markers.

Activity

1. On another sheet, you are given several patterns for folded paper objects.

2. Follow the instructions on the pattern sheet and fold paper to make the objects.

3. Find at least one book about paper folding. Try folding an object from instructions in the book or create and fold a design of your own.

4. Use one or more of the objects you've made as part of a picture you create. Use construction paper for the background of the picture.

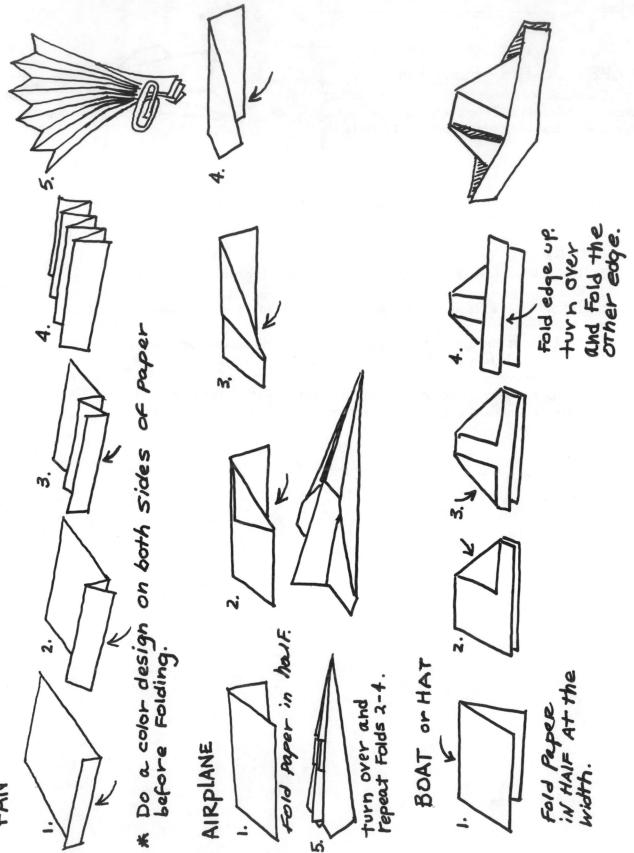

FAN

1.

2.

3.

4.

5.

* Do a color design on both sides of paper before folding.

AIRPLANE

1. Fold paper in half.

2.

3.

5. Turn over and repeat folds 2-4.

BOAT or HAT

1. Fold paper in half at the width.

2.

3.

4. Fold edge up. Turn over and fold the other edge.

Name _____

CREATIVE ART—Torn Paper Designs

Materials
Various kinds and textures of paper (scraps are fine), scissors, glue, colored paper for background.

Activity

1. Find many kinds, colors, and textures of paper.

2. In the space below, create a design or picture by tearing off and gluing pieces of paper in place. Do not use scissors or pencils. Use only torn paper and glue.

3. Cut on the line below and glue your picture onto a larger piece of colored paper.

Name _____

SOCIAL STUDIES—A Personal Litterbag

Littering, or leaving things scattered about, is not only messy, but is also costly. States and cities spend many thousands of dollars each year keeping litter cleaned from roadsides and streets. Businesses must hire people to clean up parking lots and grounds. Much of this litter is paper thrown about by careless people. You can help keep your surroundings clean and neat by always placing scrap paper in wastebaskets or garbage containers.

Materials

Plain paper bags (medium size), cord or yarn, reinforcements, paper punch, scissors, crayons or markers.

Activity

1. Fold about 1½" of the top of a bag to the outside. Fold again to make a sturdy collar around the top.

2. Punch two holes on each side of the bag through all layers of the collar. Place reinforcements around the holes both inside and outside.

3. Cut two pieces of cord or yarn, 13"-18" long depending on the size of the bag you're using. Put a length of cord through the holes on one side of the bag from the outside to the inside of the bag and tie the ends tightly on the inside. Make another handle on the opposite side of the bag.

4. Decorate your bag as you wish.

5. Use your bag to pick up litter around your desk or in the halls. Be sure to empty it in the proper place. You might want to take your litterbag home for use in your room or in the family car.

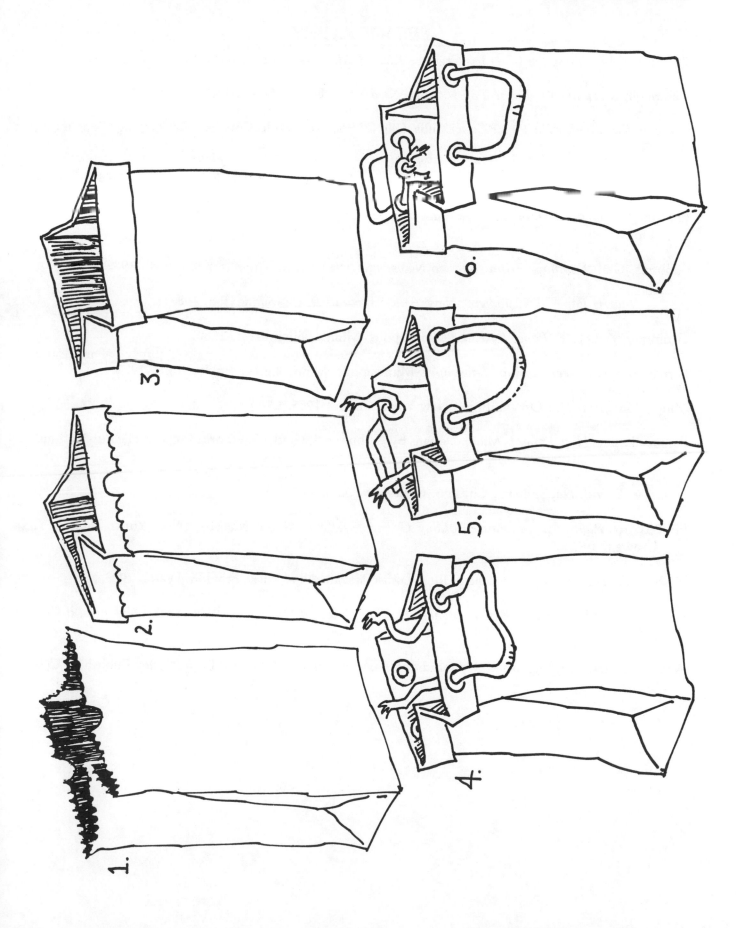

BIBLIOGRAPHY

Bottomley, Jim. *Paper Projects for Creative Kids of All Ages*. Boston: Little Brown & Co., 1983.

Campbell, Margaret W. *Paper Toy Making*. New York: Dover Publications, Inc., 1975.

Cooney, Caroline B. *The Paper Caper*. Illus. Gail Owens. New York: Coward, McCann and Geoghegan, 1981.

Cosner, Sharon. *Paper through the Ages*. Minneapolis, Minn.: Carolrhoda Books, Inc., 1984.

English, Betty Lou. *Behind the Headlines at a Big City Paper*. New York: Lothrop, Lee and Shepard Books, 1985.

Gibbons, Gail. *Deadline! From News to Newspaper*. New York: Thomas Y. Crowell, 1987.

_____. *Paper, Paper, Everywhere*. New York: Harcourt Brace Jovanovich, 1983.

Grummer, Arnold E. *Paper by Kids*. Minneapolis, Minn.: Dillon Press, 1980.

Lerner, Mark. *Careers with a Newspaper*. Minneapolis, Minn.: Lerner Publications, 1977.

Miller, Margaret. *Hot Off the Press*. New York: Crown, 1985.

Perrins, Lesley. *How Paper Is Made*. Designs by Arthur Lockwood. New York: Facts on File Publications, 1985.

Peterson, David. *Newspapers*. Chicago: Childrens Press, 1983.

Phillips, Jo. *Right Angles (Paper Folding Geometry)*. Illus. Giulio Maestro. New York: Thomas Y. Crowell, 1972.

Pitcher, Caroline. *Planes and Space*. Illus. Louise Nevatt. New York: Franklin Watts, 1983.

Smith, Elizabeth Simpson. *Paper: Inventions That Changed Our Lives*. New York: Walker and Co., 1984.

Weiss, Harvey. *Working with Cardboard and Paper*. Reading, Mass.: Addison-Wesley Publishing Co., 1978.

ANSWER KEY

FROM TREE TO PAPER

1. Trees are sawed in the forest.

2. The bark is removed.

3. The wood is cut into chips.

4. The chips are cooked.

5. The cooked pulp is drained and washed.

6. The pulp is pressed into sheets.

7. The paper is dried.

8. The paper is wound into huge rolls.

Time

OBJECTIVES

To help students learn the history of telling time.

To help students become aware of how time affects their daily lives.

MATERIALS

Crayons and/or markers, scissors, glue, paper, pencils, rulers or yardsticks, lined paper, paper fasteners, paper punches, chalk.

TOPIC OF THE WEEK

This introductory activity is to be used with the class as a whole as an introduction to the unit. To allow the students time to read and gather information, it should be used a day or more before they go to Day's End Areas. Encourage them to share their word associations.

DAY'S END AREAS

Telling Time with Roman Numerals

The students will make pockets and cut out time cards with which to practice telling time with Roman numeral clock faces.

Duplicate the pocket pattern on construction paper.

History and Art—Ways of Telling Time

The students will research to learn the ways people have told time from very early times to the present and will make illustrated time lines showing this information.

(Wide adding machine paper works well for this activity.)

Scheduling Time—My Day's Schedule

The students will make schedules showing their activities for the day and how they plan to use the time during the rest of the day and evening.

Art and Writing—Future Time

The children will write descriptions and make illustrations or models of what they imagine clocks or time-telling devices will be like a hundred years from now.